Dear Family Member,

Sight words are those frequently used, non-decodable words that are essential to reading fluency. Ask any teacher or educational expert what's the only way for children to master these sight words and they'll all agree—practice!

We've created the *Scholastic 100 Words* workbook series to give your child that practice. Working with literacy specialists and classroom teachers, we identified the 100 sight words your child needs to know by first grade. Then we developed inviting educational activities to give your child opportunities to read, write, and use these words.

The sight words in *Scholastic's 100 Words Kids Need to Read by 1st Grade* are divided into six word groups. The words in each group are introduced in context and reinforced throughout the activities. As your child moves through this workbook, he or she will move from visual recognition of sight words to genuine mastery. Your child will also gain important preparatory experience that will later help with standardized tests.

To reinforce the message that skill-building helps make reading fluent—*and fun*—we've included a wonderful "mini-book" at the end of each word group section. This mini-book weaves all the words from the word group into a lively story your child will love reading aloud. And to encourage your child's love of reading, we've also included a poster listing 100 Great Books for 1st Graders.

The journey through these workbook pages will help young readers make the successful transition from learning to read to reading to learn. Enjoy the trip!

David Goddy
Publisher, Scholastic Magazines

Tips For Family Members

Join in with your child on the activity pages:
✓ Read the directions aloud.
✓ Help your child get started by making sure he or she knows what to do.
✓ Point out examples, such as circles or underlines, in the directions. Show your child how to use the illustrations or photos to provide clues for words.

Share the mini-books with your child:
✓ To assemble a mini-book, detach the two pages where perforated. Fold first sheet at dotted line so that pages 1 and 8 of mini-book are on the outside, and pages 2 and 7 are on the inside. Fold second sheet so that pages 3 and 6 are on the outside, and pages 4 and 5 are on the inside. Insert second folded sheet into first folded sheet. The mini-book cover will be on the outside and story pages will follow in number order.
✓ Ask your child to read the story aloud to you. Using the word list on page 3, ask your child to find all the words from the word group in the mini-book.

Read, read, read!
✓ Visit your library or bookstore and help your child find the 100 Great Books for 1st Graders listed on our poster.

Table of Contents

Editorial Consultant: Mary C. Rose, Orange County Public Schools, Orlando Florida • **Writers:** Lisa Trumbauer; Anne Schreiber; Gail Tuchman; Kathryn McKeon; **Illustrators:** Valeria Petrone; Greg Paprocki; Jackie Snider; **Art Director:** Nancy Sabato; **Composition:** Kevin Callahan, BNGO Books; **Cover:** Red Herring Design

My 100 Words

Group 1

a	girl	little
an	goes	she
as	has	the
at	he	to
boy	is	was
by	it	

Group 2

am	jump	play
down	me	ran
fast	my	run
have	off	up
I	on	in
	out	

Group 3

and	friend	they
are	good	we
did	had	were
do	mother	yes
don't	no	you
father	not	

Group 4

ate	if	sit
be	look	stop
day	night	went
eat	of	will
for	rain	with
from	sat	

Group 5

black	green	see
blue	new	that
book	old	this
can	orange	want
car	red	yellow
go	saw	

Group 6

came	get	six
come	give	ten
eight	got	three
five	nine	two
four	one	
gave	seven	

I Saw a . . .

Circle the word **a** in each sentence.

I saw a bird.

I saw a bird in a tree.

I saw a bird in a tree with a bug.

I saw a bird in a tree with a bug on a leaf.

Write the word **a** on the lines below.

I saw _____

in _____

with _____

on _____ .

Making Words

Make words by following the directions.

1. Write the word **a**.

   Add the letter **t** at the end. _____

   What word did you make? _____

2. Write the word **a**.

   Add the letter **n** at the end. _____

   What word did you make? _____

3. Write the word **a**.

   Add the letter **s** at the end. _____

   What word did you make? _____

Circle the words you made above in the story below. Hint: One word is written with a capital **A**.

An ant found a cookie.

The cookie was as big as the ant!

The ant ate the cookie at home.

Mystery Animal

Find all the words that start with the letter **a**.
Color those spaces orange.
You will find an animal hiding in the picture.

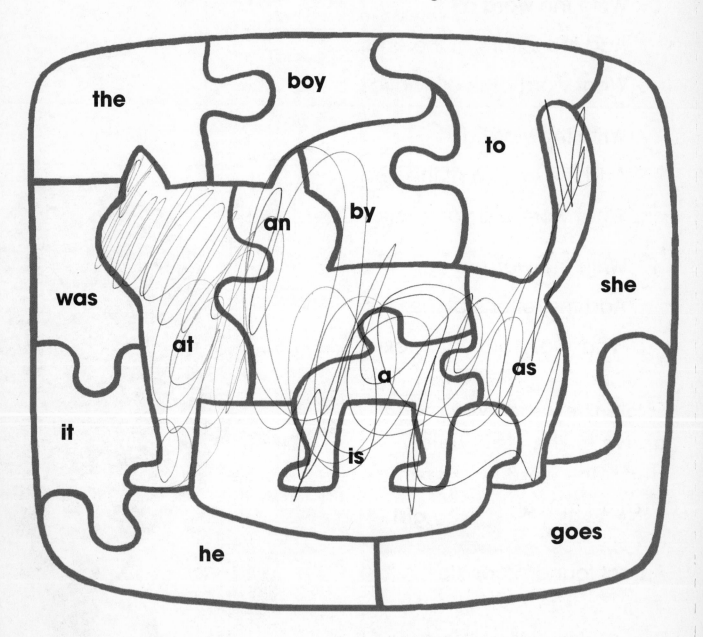

Cross the Stream

Help the fawn cross the stream to its mother.
Color all the stones in the stream
that have words that start with the letter **a**.

Word Maze

Help the dog find its bone. Follow a path through the maze. Follow the path that has only words that begin with the letter **a**.

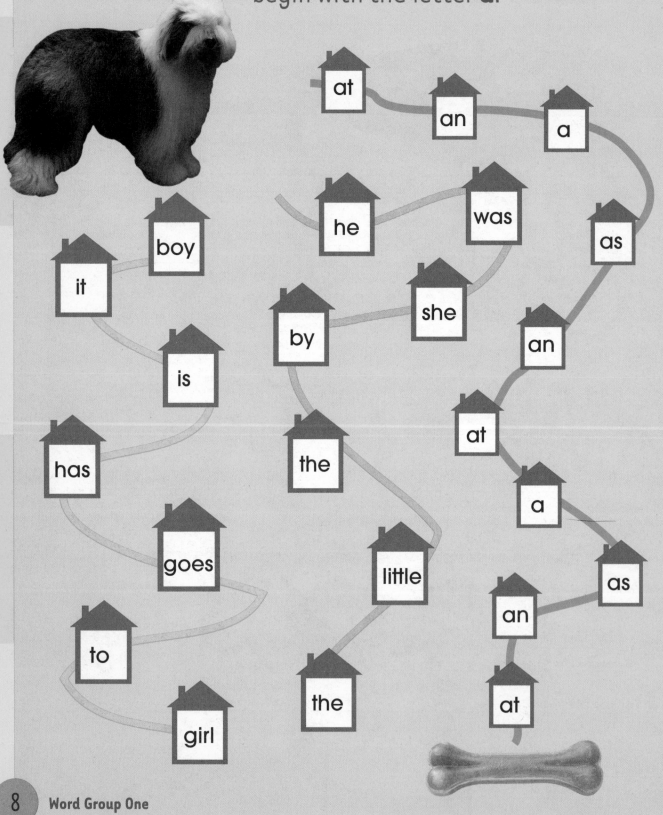

Climb the Castle

Help the knight climb the castle wall to reach the princess. Color in the squares that have the word **the**.

Where Is It?

Circle the word (the) in each sentence.
Write the word **the** on the line.

_____
- - - - - - - - - - -

The bee is on _____ flower.

_____
- - - - - - - - - - -

The cat is in _____ window.

_____
- - - - - - - - - - -

The birds are in _____ nest.

_____
- - - - - - - - - - -

The lizard is on _____ rock.

I See

Draw a line to match the
pictures to the sentences.

I see a duck.

The duck is brown.

I see a cat.

The cat is black.

I see a dog.

The dog is black.

I see a bird.

The bird is red.

I see a frog.

The frog is green.

Circle the word (a).
Draw a square around the word The.

What's the Weather?

Answer the questions by writing the word **The** on the lines.

What kind of day is it?

_____

- - - - - - - - - - -

_____ day is cloudy.

What kind of day is it?

_____

- - - - - - - - - - -

_____ day is snowy.

What kind of day is it?

_____

- - - - - - - - - - - -

_____ day is windy.

What kind of day is it?

_____

- - - - - - - - - - -

_____ day is sunny.

What kind of day is it?

_____

- - - - - - - - - -

_____ day is rainy.

Who Is It?

Circle the correct word
to complete the sentence.

The (girl, boy) is writing.

The (girl, boy) is reading a book.

The (girl, boy) is jumping rope.

The (girl, boy) is blowing bubbles.

The (girl, boy) is climbing a tree.

Which One?

Write **boy** or **girl** to show
who is in the picture.

_____

- - - - - - - - - - -

_____

_____

- - - - - - - - - - -

_____

_____

- - - - - - - - - - -

_____

_____

- - - - - - - - - - -

_____

What About You?

Draw a picture of yourself in the picture frame.

Are you a boy or a girl?
Write the word **boy** or **girl** on the line
to complete the first sentence.
Write your name on the next line
to complete the second sentence.

_____

- -

I am a _____ .

_____

- -

My name is _____ .

Color the Animal

Color in the spaces to see the animal.
Use the colors below.

If the word is **girl**, color the space orange.
If the word is **boy**, color the space black.
If the word starts with **a** or **t**, color the space green.

Lunch!

Circle the word (girl). Circle the word (She).
Draw a square around the word [boy].
Draw a square around
the word [He].

The boy drinks milk.

He drinks milk.

The girl eats lunch.

She eats a lunch.

The boy eats an apple.

He eats an apple.

The girl eats a sandwich.

She eats a sandwich.

Take a Trip

The boy is taking a trip.

_____

- - - - - - - -

_____ is taking a trip.

The boy rides in a car.

_____

- - - - - - - -

_____ rides in a car.

The boy packs a bag.

_____

- - - - - - - -

_____ packs a bag.

The boy packs a lunch.

_____

- - - - - - - -

_____ packs a lunch.

The boy eats lunch in the car.

_____

- - - - - - - -

_____ eats lunch in the car.

Put on a Play

Write the word **She** on the lines.

The girl is putting on a show.

_____

- - - - - - - - - -

_____ is putting on a show.

The girl sings.

_____

- - - - - - - - - -

_____ sings.

The girl dances.

_____

- - - - - - - - - -

_____ dances.

The girl acts.

_____

- - - - - - - - - -

_____ acts.

The girl takes a bow.

_____

- - - - - - - - - -

_____ takes a bow.

Secret Message!

Write the correct word on the line. Use the words in the box. (Hint: You can use some words more than once!)

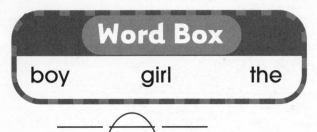

Word Box

boy   girl   the

1. _____ _____ day was cloudy.

2. _____ _____ secret plan was still a go.

3. The _____ _____ _____ read the note. She had the map.

4. The _____ _____ _____ walked to the tree house.

5. She met a _____ _____ there.

6. They read the note together.

Now write the circled letters in order on the lines below to read the secret message.

_____ _____ _____ _____ _____

_____ _____ _____ _____ _____

Who Is It?

Read each question.
Answer the question by writing **It** and **is** on the lines.

Knock, knock! Who is it?

_____ _____

- - - - - - - - - - -

Moo! _____ _____ a cow.

Knock, knock! Who is it?

_____ _____

- - - - - - - - - - -

Oink! _____ _____ a pig.

Knock, knock! Who is it?

_____ _____

- - - - - - - - - - -

Quack! _____ _____ a duck.

Knock, knock! Who is it?

_____ _____

- - - - - - - - - - -

Baaa! _____ _____ a sheep.

Color It

Write the word **it** on the lines. Color the balloons.

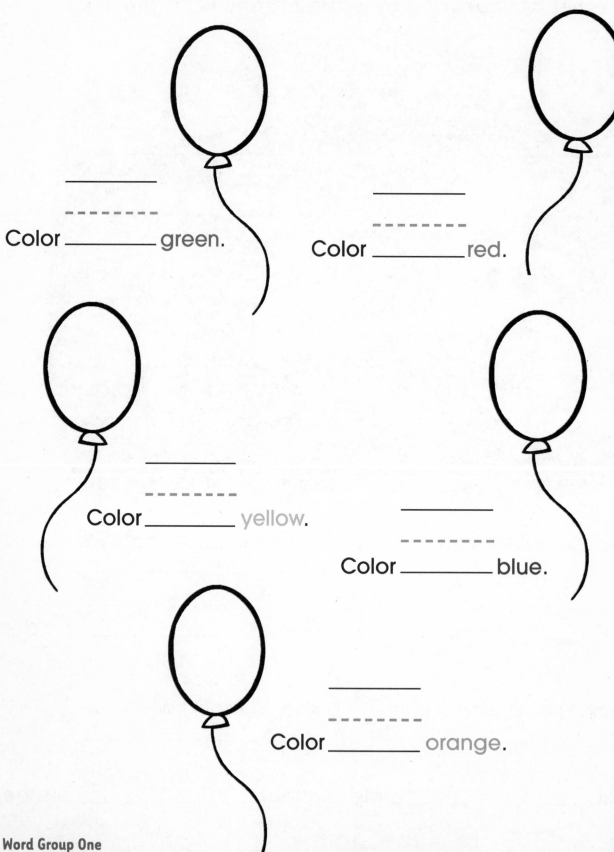

Color _____ green.

Color _____ red.

Color _____ yellow.

Color _____ blue.

Color _____ orange.

I See It!

Draw a line to match the sentence with the insect.

I see a bee!

It is on a flower.

I see an ant!

It is on a leaf.

I see a ladybug!

It is on a leaf, too.

I see a beetle.

It is in the grass.

Circle the word (It). Draw a square around the word [is]. Draw a triangle around the word /a\. Draw one line under the word __an__. Draw two lines under the word <u><u>the</u></u>.

What Are They Doing?

Write the word **boy** or **girl** and the word **is**
to finish the sentences.

_____ _____

The _____ _____ planting flowers.

_____ _____

The _____ _____ walking the dog.

_____ _____

The _____ _____ making cookies.

_____ _____

The _____ _____ swimming in the pool.

Unlock the Secret!

Find the key that matches the word in each lock. Do you see another letter on the key? Write the letters in order on the numbered lines. Then read the secret message!

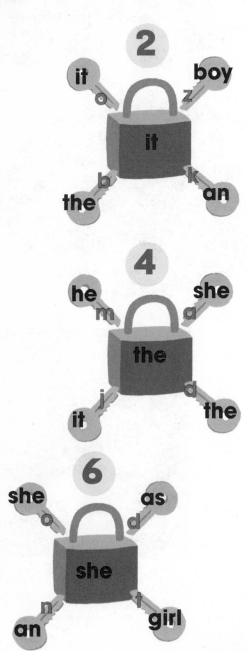

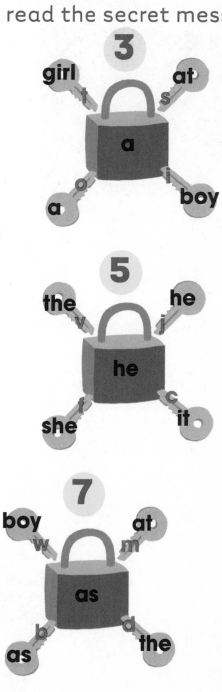

_____   _____

- - - - - - - - - - - - - - - - - - -   - - - - - - - - - - - -

_____   _____
 1   2   3   4   5   6   7

Who Has It?

Write the number next to the picture that answers the question.

1. Who has the cat?

2. Who has the cookie?

3. Who has the puppy?

4. Who has the book?

5. Who has the doll?

Circle the word (has) in each question.

Jan's Day

It is morning! Jan goes to school.

It is noon! Jan goes to lunch.

It is afternoon! Jan goes out to play.

It is evening! Jan goes to her room.

It is night! Jan goes to sleep.

Write the word **goes** on the lines.

_____

What does Jan do first? Jan _____ to school.

_____

What does Jan do next? Jan _____ to lunch.

_____

What does Jan do then? Jan _____ out to play.

_____

What does Jan do next? Jan _____to her room.

_____

What does Jan do last? Jan _____ to sleep.

Find the Frog

Help the boy and girl find their frog.
Follow the maze path that has the words **goes to** in it.

At the Fair

Circle the word that tells who is in the picture. Write the words **goes to** on the lines.

_____ _____

- - - - - - - - - - - - - - - - - - -

(She, He) _____ _____ the fun park.

_____ _____

- - - - - - - - - - - - - - - - - -

(She, He) _____ _____ the games.

_____ _____

- - - - - - - - - - - - - - - - - -

(She, He) _____ _____ the candy stand.

_____ _____

- - - - - - - - - - - - - - - - -

(She, He)_____ _____ see the animals.

Yeah, Team!

Find the team. Circle the players that have the word **goes** on their shirts.

Tell Me a Riddle

Draw a line to the picture
to answer the riddle.

What has wings and goes in the air?

What has wheels and goes on a track?

What has wheels and goes on a road?

What has sails and goes on the water?

Find the word **has** in each riddle. Circle it.
Find the word **goes** in each riddle. Underline it.

Word Sense

Circle the word that makes the most sense.

1. The girl (has, goes) a present.

She (has, goes) to a party.

2. The boy (has, goes) a sled.

He (has, goes) to the hill.

3. The girl (has, goes) a dog.

She (has, goes) to the park.

4. The boy (has, goes) a pail.

He (has, goes) to the beach.

Feed the Kitten

Color the tiles on the floor that have the word **by** on them. The colored tiles will lead the kitten to the milk.

by	by	boy	it	goes
an	by	the	was	girl
she	by	by	little	boy
he	has	by	the	to
girl	as	by	at	was
boy	she	by	by	by

Lots of Littles

Write the word **little** on the line to tell about the pictures.

This house is big.

_____

This house is _____ .

This truck is big.

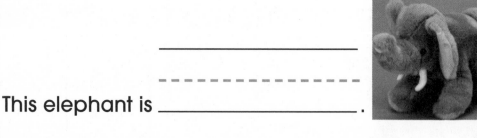

_____

This truck is _____ .

This elephant is big.

_____

This elephant is _____ .

This clown is big.

_____

This clown is _____ .

Write a Poem

Write the word **little** on the lines to finish the poem.

_____

- - - - - - - - - - - - - - -

I saw a _____ flower.

_____

- - - - - - - - - - - - - - -

I saw a _____ bee.

_____

- - - - - - - - - - - - - - -

I saw a _____ bird.

_____

- - - - - - - - - - - - - - -

It flew over_____ me!

Draw a picture for the poem in the box.

Water World

Help the boat sail across the ocean.
Complete each sentence in the path with the correct word.
The words in the box will help you.

Word Box

is	has	It
The	to	goes
little	by	as
an		

_____

Our ship _____ in the water.

_____

I saw _____ octopus!

_____

A whale _____ swimming beside us.

_____

The whale is _____ big as our ship!

_____

Our ship sails _____ the island.

_____

_____ sun feels very warm.

_ you see the dolphin?

_____

_____ leaped out of the water.

_____

Our ship sails _____ a seal!

_____

The shark _____ sharp teeth.

_____

I saw a _____ fish in the water!

4 circle **a** 10 times; write **a** 4 times

5 at, an, as; circle an; as, as; at

6 a cat

7 color the following stones: a, an, as, a, at, an

8 correct maze path follows words with **a**

9 color **the** 7 times

10 circle **The** 4 times; write **the** four times

11 draw lines to match photos to text; circle **a** 5 times; draw a square around **The** 5 times

12 write **The** 5 times

13 girl; boy; girl; girl; boy

14 boy; girl; girl; boy; boy

15 answers will vary

16 a tiger

17 circle **girl** and **she** 2 times each; draw a square around **boy** and **he** 2 times each

18 write **He** 5 times

19 write **She** 5 times

20 The; The; girl; girl; boy; hello

21 write the words **It is** 4 times

22 write the word **it** 5 times

23 draw lines to match text to photos; circle **It** 4 times; draw a square around **is** 4 times; draw a triangle around **a** 6 times; underline **an** 1 time; draw two lines under **the** 1 time

24 girl is; boy is; boy is; girl is

25 good job

26 top to bottom: 4, 2, 1, 3, 5; circle **has** 5 times

27 write **goes** 5 times

28 maze path follows **goes to**

29 circle: She; He; She; He; write **goes to** 4 times

30 circle 7 players **goes**

31 draw lines to match text to photos; circle **has** 4 times; underline **goes** 4 times

32 has, goes; has, goes; has, goes; has, goes

33 draw lines to match questions to photos: airplane with sheet of paper; cookie with flour, sugar, and eggs; flower with seed; house to the wood

34–35 write **was** 8 times

36 write **by** 5 times

37 color **by** 10 times

38 write **little** 4 times

39 write **little** 4 times

40–41 goes or is; an; is; as; to; The; It; by; has; little

They end up at their bikes.

Safe! Tag is over.

The girl gets on her bike.

The boy gets on his bike.

They do not go fast.

They are too tired!

But it was fun to play at the park!

8

fold & assemble

Bikes at the Park

by Anne Schreiber

Illustrated by Jackie Snider

Scholastic 100 Words Kids Need to Read by 1st Grade, Word Group 1

1

The boy goes this way.

The girl goes that way.

The boy goes that way.

The girl goes this way.

7

The girl has a bike.

It is a little bike, but it can go fast.

Zoom! The girl on the bike goes fast.

Zoom! Zoom! She goes past a boy.

2

The girl is IT.
She has to tag the boy.
They run and run.
The girl is as fast as the boy.
She tags him.
Now the boy is IT.

The boy sees the girl go by.
The boy has a bike, too.
He goes to get it.

The girl goes to the park.

She gets off her bike.

The boy goes to the park, too.

He gets off his bike.

They play tag.

It is an old bike, but it can go fast.

Zoom! The boy goes fast.

Zoom! Zoom! He goes after the girl.

I Have

Write the word **I** on the line to finish the sentence.

____
____ have two [hands].

____
____ have two

____
____ have two [head].

____
____ have two [feet].

____
____ have two [eyes].

But there is only one me!

Here I am.

Draw a picture of yourself in the picture frame. Write your name on the line.

_____

- -

I am _____!

I Am

Write the word **I** on the line.

____
\- \- \- \-

1. ____ am happy.

____
\- \- \- \-

2. ____ am sad.

____
\- \- \- \-

3. ____ am sleepy.

____
\- \- \- \-

4. ____ am hungry.

____
\- \- \- \-

5. ____ am hot.

Match the sentence with the children in the picture.
Write the number of the sentence next to the correct child.

Animal Actions

Draw a line to match the
sentence with each animal.

I am swimming.

I am hopping.

I am flying.

I am running.

I am sleeping.

Circle the word (I) in each
sentence. Underline the
word **am** in each sentence.

Flying Home

Help the space creature fly home. Draw a line connecting the words **I** and **am** to get to the planet.

Where Am I?

Write the words **I am** on the lines. Draw a line to match the sentence with the picture.

Where am I?

_____ _____

_____ _____ at home.

Where am I?

_____ _____

_____ _____ on the bus.

Where am I?

_____ _____

_____ _____ at school.

Where am I?

_____ _____

_____ _____ at the playground.

Where am I?

_____ _____

_____ _____ in the tree!

Party Planners

Match the sentences with the children in the picture.
Write the number of the sentence next to the correct child.

1. I have the cake.

2. I have the balloons.

3. I have the gifts.

4. I have the juice.

Circle the word (I) in each sentence.

Underline the word **have** in each sentence.

What Do I Have?

Color the spaces with the word **have**.
The picture will show you what is in the box.

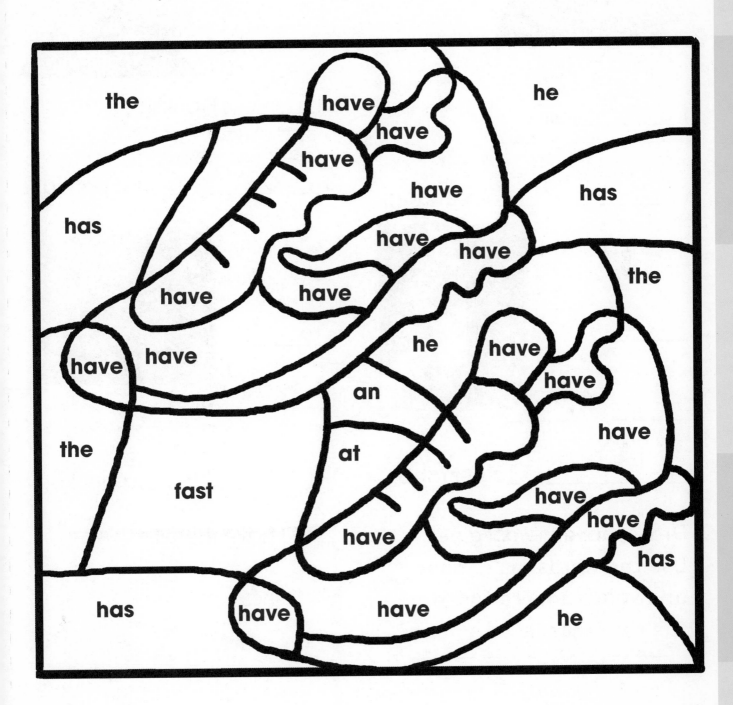

Meet Our Pets

Use the words **am** or **have**
to finish the sentences.

_____

I _____ Julie.

I _____ a pet dog.

_____

I _____ Anna.

I _____ a pet rabbit.

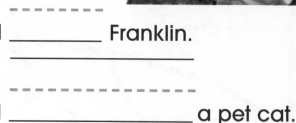

_____

I _____ Franklin.

I _____ a pet cat.

_____

I _____ Jake.

I _____ a pet frog.

Draw yourself with a pet.
Use the words **am** or **have**
and your name to finish
the sentences.

_____ _____

I _____ _____ .

I _____ a pet.

Animals of Africa

Circle the correct word for each sentence.

I (am, have) an elephant.

I (am, have) a trunk.

I (am, have) a zebra.
I (am, have) stripes.

I (am, have) a giraffe.

I (am, have) a long neck.

I (am, have) a lion.

I (am, have) a mane.

About You

Complete each sentence to tell about you.

_____

- -

My name is _____ .

_____

- -

My birthday is _____ .

_____

- -

My favorite food is _____ .

_____

- -

My favorite color is _____ .

_____

- -

My favorite toy is _____ .

Circle the word (My) in each sentence.

Draw a picture of your favorite animal.

Lost Cat!

Help me find my cat!
Follow the path that
has the word **my** in it.

go

she

at my

its

am

my

me

my

am man

my

have

my

to

I my me

man my was

was my I

am my

Meet Andrew!

Write the word **my** on the lines.

Hi! I am Andrew!

Here are some of _____ things!

This is _____ ball.

This is _____ car.

This is _____ fish.

This is _____ kite.

This is _____ sister.

This is my _____ family.

Do You See Me?

Write the number of the sentence next to the correct animal.

1. I am eating grass.

Do you see me?

2. I am eating an acorn.

Do you see me?

3. I am eating berries.

Do you see me?

4. I am eating a flower.

Do you see me?

Circle the word (I) in each sentence.

Draw a square around the word me in each sentence.

Let's Talk!

Write the word **me** on the lines.

I talk to the policewoman.
_____

- - - - - - - -

She talks to _____ .

I talk to the mailman.
_____

- - - - - - - -

He talks to _____ .

I talk to the teacher.
_____

- - - - - - - -

She talks to _____ .

I talk to the pizza man.
_____

- - - - - - - -

He talks to _____ .

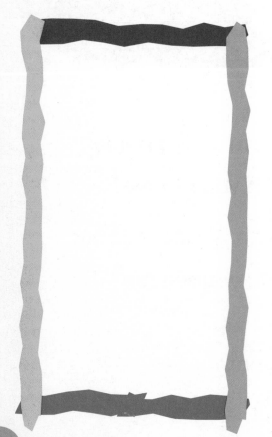

Who do you talk to?
Draw a person you talk to.
Write the word **me** and circle the correct word to finish the sentence.
_____

- - - - - - - -

(He, she) talks to _____ .

Fruit Salad

Draw a line to match the fruits and sentences.

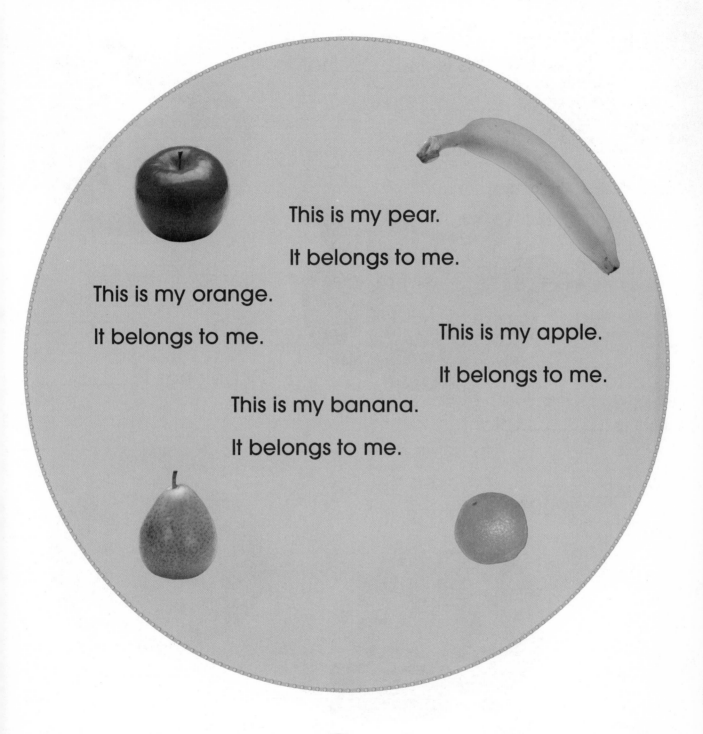

This is my pear.

It belongs to me.

This is my orange.

It belongs to me.

This is my apple.

It belongs to me.

This is my banana.

It belongs to me.

Circle the word **my** in each sentence.
Underline **me** in each sentence.

My and Me

This is _____ hat.

It belongs to _____ .

This is _____ box.

It belongs to _____ .

This is _____ plant.

It belongs to _____ .

This is _____ bag.

It belongs to _____ .

This is _____ drum.

It belongs to _____ .

Making Words

Follow the directions to make the words below.

_____

- - - - - - - - - - - - -

1. Write the word **a**.   _____

_____

- - - - - - - - - - - - -

2. Add the letter **m** to the end.   _____

3. Take off the **a**, and add   _____

- - - - - - - - - - - - -

   the letter **y** to the end.   _____

4. Take off the **y**, and add   _____

- - - - - - - - - - - - -

   the letter **e** to the end.   _____

Complete these sentences with the words you wrote above.

_____
- - - -

I see _____ butterfly.

_____
- - - - - - - - -

I _____ happy!

_____
- - - - - - - -

_____ cat chases the butterfly.

_____
- - - - - - -

My cat comes back to _____ .

Who's Hiding? Find out who is hiding.

Color the spaces with the word **my** black.

Color the spaces with the word **me** red.

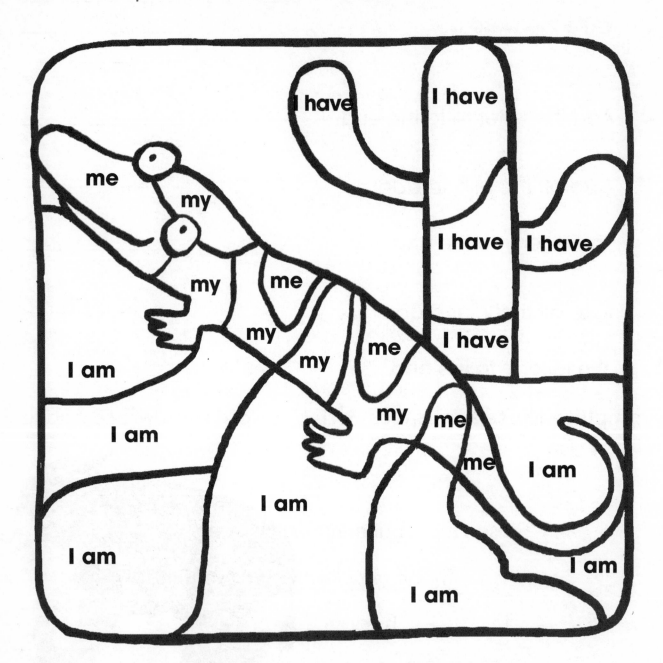

Finish the picture.

Color the spaces with the words **I am** brown.

Color the spaces with the words **I have** green.

From Me to You

Complete the poem.
Circle the correct word **I**, **my**, or **me**.

(I, my, me) have a little secret,

a secret of (I, my, me) own.

(I, my, me) want to share it with you,

in (I, my, me) little poem.

It is something special to (I, my, me).

It is something that (I, my, me) love.

It is something special from (I, my, me).

It is called (I, my, me) little hug.

Save the Prince!

Help save the prince!
Color a path from the princess to the prince.
Color the squares with the words **I**, **my**, and **me**.

I	me	he	she	have
was	my	by	at	boy
girl	I	am	little	goes
have	me	me	am	to
the	a	I	was	is
it	have	I	my	me

At the Playground

Write the number of the sentence
next to the correct child.

[ ]

[ ]

1. I run on the grass.

2. I play on the bars.

3. I jump off the swing.

[ ]

Circle the word (I).
Underline the word that tells an action.

Run, Jump, Play

Write the word **I** on each line.
Underline the word that tells what you like to do.

____
- - - -
____ like to run.

____
- - - -
____ like to play.

____
- - - -
____ like to jump.

In each box, draw a picture of yourself
doing what the sentence says.

At the Beach

I like to go to the beach!

I like to play in the sand.

I like to jump in the waves.

I like to run in the water.

The beach is fun!

Answer the questions.
Write the correct action word on the line.

What does the boy like to do in the water?

_____

- - - - - - - - - -

He likes to _____ .

What does the boy like to do in the sand?

_____

- - - - - - - - - - -

He likes to _____ .

What does the boy like to do in the waves?

_____

- - - - - - - - - -

He likes to _____ .

A New Game

Here is a new game! First, you run as fast as you can across the field.

Next, you jump as high as you can to reach a tree branch.

The person who touches the branch last is **it**. Then you play a game of tag.

Explain how to play the game. Write the correct action word on the line. Hint: You may have to use capital letters.

_____

- - - - - - - - - - -

1. _____ as fast as you can.

_____

- - - - - - - - - - - - - -

2. _____ as high as you can.

_____

- - - - - - - - - - - - - -

3. _____ a game of tag.

Puzzle Page

Complete each sentence with a word from the box. Write the words in the puzzle.

Word Box

have   jump   me   play   run   My

Words to Write Across:

2. I ____ up.

4. ___ dog has fur.

5. I ____ a pet cat.

Words to Write Down:

1. I ___ across the grass.

3. I ___ with my friends.

4. The dog belongs to ___ .

I like to run!

Run, Rover, Run!

Write the word **run** on each first line.
Write the word **ran** on each second line.

_____

- - - - - - - - - - -

Today, I _____ in the yard.

_____

- - - - - - - - - -

Yesterday, I _____ in the yard, too!

_____

- - - - - - - - - -

Today, I _____ around the flowers.

_____

- - - - - - - - - -

Yesterday, I _____ around the flowers, too!

_____

- - - - - - - - - -

Today, I _____ in the water.

_____

- - - - - - - - - -

Yesterday, I _____ in the water, too!

_____

- - - - - - - - - -

Today, I _____ in the house.

_____

- - - - - - - - - -

Yesterday, I _____ in the house, too!

I Ran Fast!

Today, I run fast!

I run fast down the street.

I run fast across the yard.

I run fast up the hill.

I run fast down the hill, too!

What about yesterday?
Write the word **ran** on the lines
to tell how the cat ran yesterday.

_____

- - - - - - - - - -

Yesterday, I_____ fast!

_____

- - - - - - - - -

I_____ fast down the street.

_____

- - - - - - - - - -

I_____ fast across the yard.

_____

- - - - - - - - - -

I_____ fast up the hill.

_____

- - - - - - - - - -

I_____ fast down the hill, too!

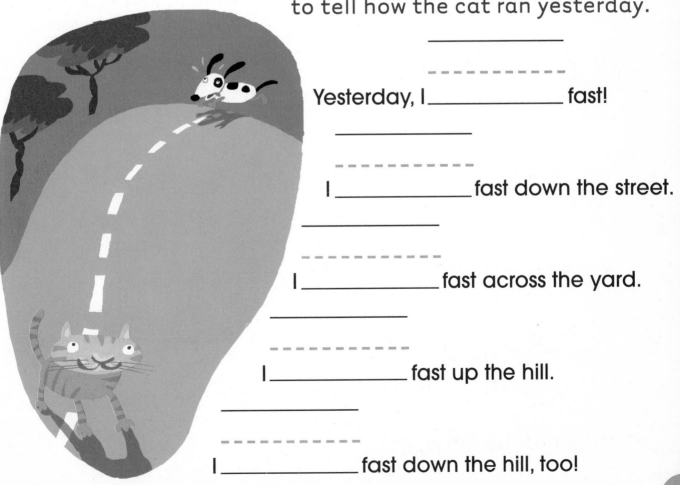

Fast Rabbit,

Write the word **fast** on the lines to complete the story.

The turtle and the rabbit were having a race.

_____

- - - - - - - - - - - - -

"I am very _____ ," said the rabbit. "I will win."

_____

- - - - - - - - - - - - -

"I am not very _____ ," said the turtle. "I am slow.

But I will still win."

_____

- - - - - - - - - - - - -

The race began. The rabbit was _____ .

He hopped down the path. The turtle was slow.

He crawled down the path.

Slow Turtle

_____

- - - - - - - - - - - - -

"I am very_____ ," said the rabbit. "I will win.

I have time for a quick nap." The rabbit fell asleep

_____

- - - - - - - - - - - - -

very _____ .

_____

- - - - - - - - - - - -

"I am not very_____ ," said the turtle. "I am slow.

But I will win." The turtle crawled down the path. He crawled past

the rabbit. The rabbit was still asleep.

_____

- - - - - - - - - - -

The turtle won the race. "I am not very_____ ," said

the turtle. "I am slow. But I keep going."

Up and Down

Look at each picture.

Write the word **up** or **down** to complete the sentence.

_____

I go _____.

_____

I go _____.

_____

I go _____.

_____

I go _____.

Eek! A Mouse!

Tell where the mouse is.
Circle the correct word in each sentence.

The mouse is (in, on) the shoe.

The mouse is (in, on) the book.

The mouse is (in, on) the rug.

The mouse is (in, on) the table.

The mouse is (in, on) the box.

The mouse is (in, on) the hole.

Insects In or Out?

Write the word **in** or **out** to tell about the insects.

Which bee is in?
Which bee is out?

_____   _____
- - - - - - - - - -   - - - - - - - - - -
_____   _____

Which ant is in?
Which ant is out?

_____   _____
- - - - - - - - - -   - - - - - - - - - -
_____   _____

Which grasshopper is in? Which grasshopper is out?

_____   _____
- - - - - - - - - -   - - - - - - - - - -
_____   _____

Fast Freddie

Freddie is fast! Write the words **on** or **off** to tell what Fast Freddie does.

Freddie jumps _____ the rock.

Freddie jumps _____ the rock.

Freddie jumps _____ the lily.

Freddie jumps _____ the lily.

Freddie jumps _____ the turtle.

Freddie jumps _____ the turtle.

That Freddie is fast!

Picking Apples

Find the words in the apple tree that begin with the same letter. Write those words in the correct basket.

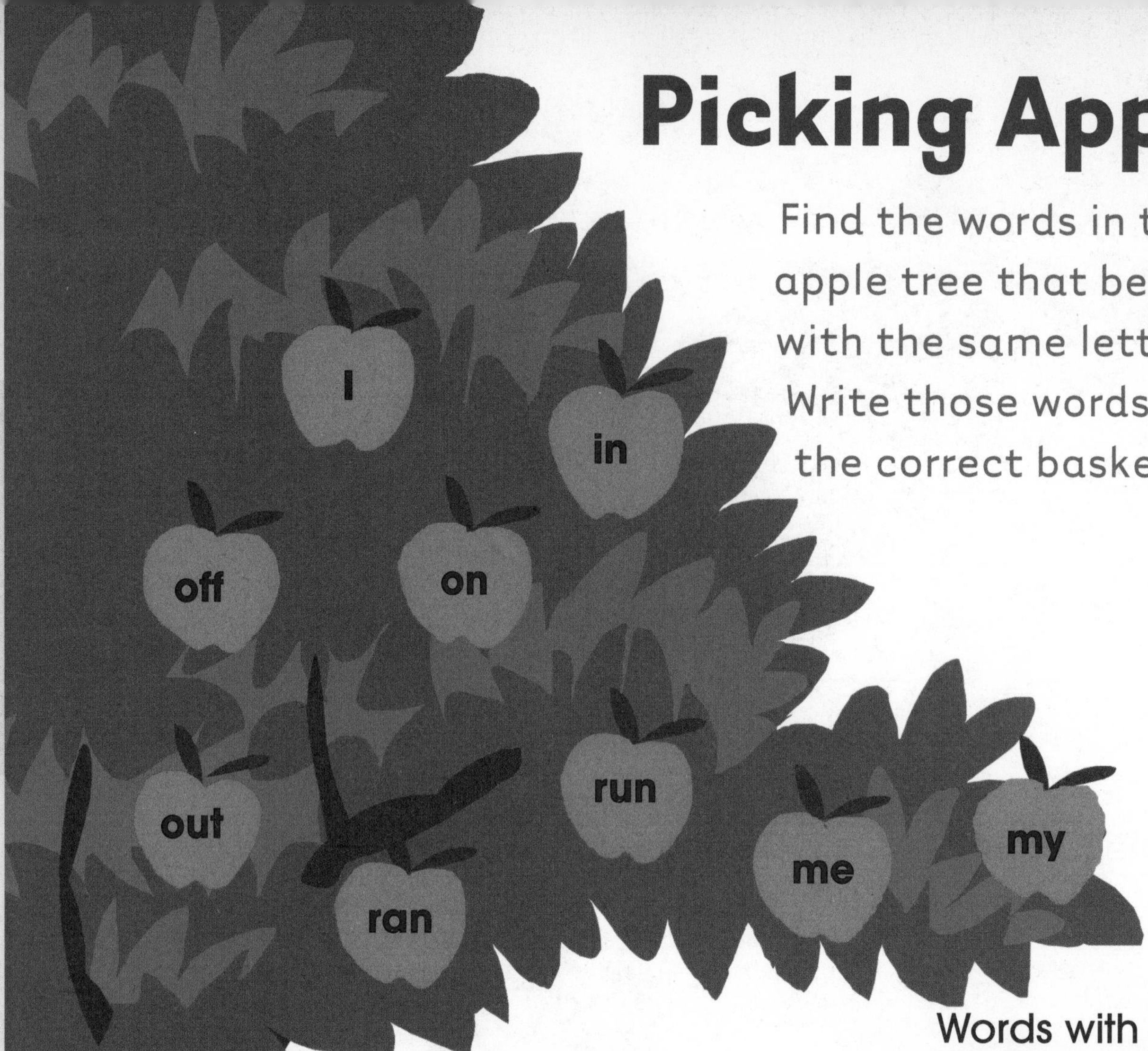

I

in

off

on

out

run

ran

me

my

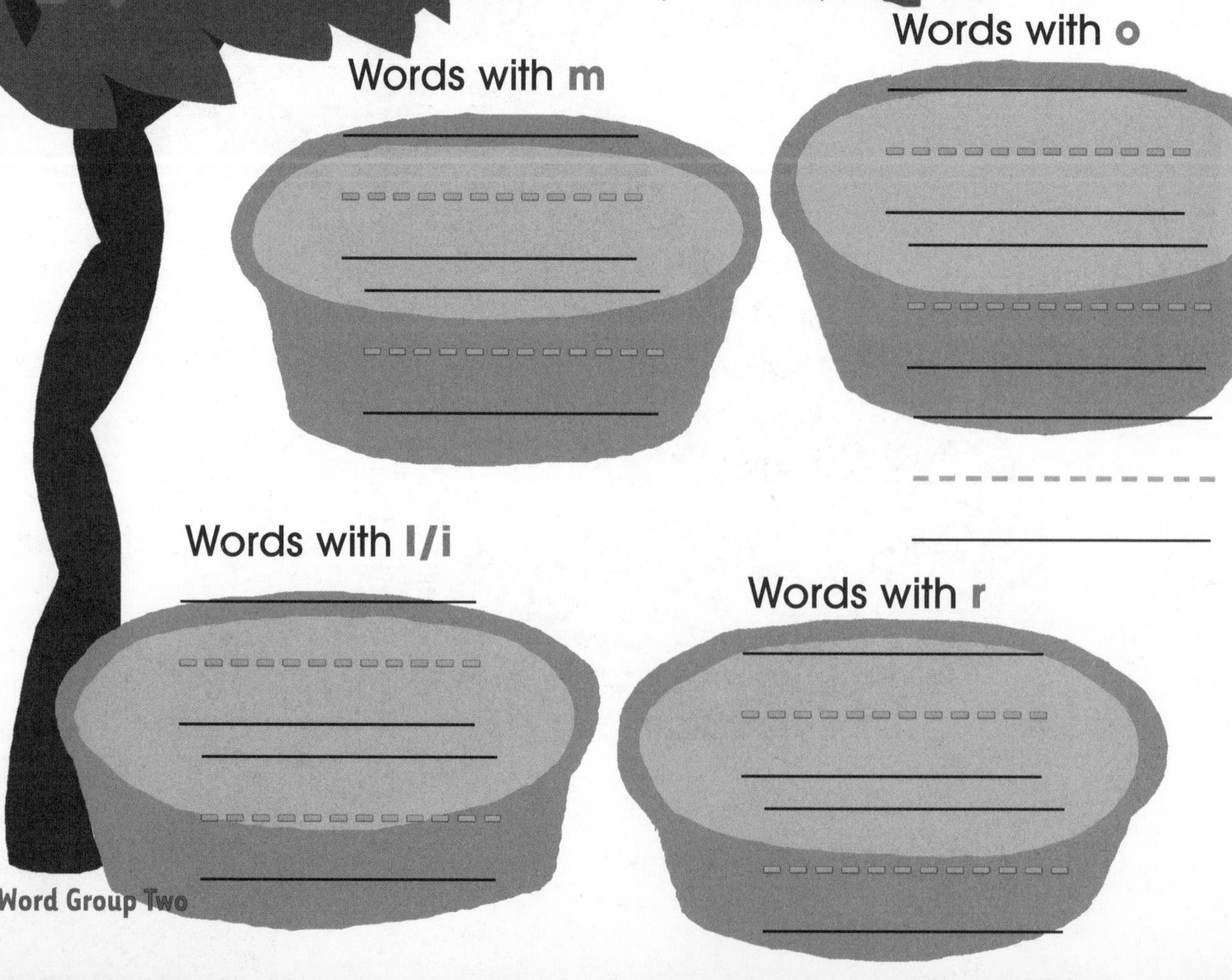

Words with **m**

Words with **o**

Words with **I/i**

Words with **r**

Hidden Message!

Find the words in the puzzle. Circle them.

Word Box

am	fast	me	out	up
down	jump	off	play	

y	j	u	m	p	o
u	d	p	l	a	y
m	e	i	o	f	f
d	i	d	o	w	n
f	a	s	t	u	p
t	o	u	t	a	m

Write the letters you did **not** circle on the lines in order.

___ ___ ___   ___ ___ ___   ___ ___

- -

___ ___ ___ ___   ___ ___ ___ !

The Case of the Missing Jewels

The museum jewels are missing!
Unlock each room to find the missing jewels.
The missing letter for each room is the same.
Hint: It's not the letter in the jewel!
Figure out the missing letters and write them on the lines.

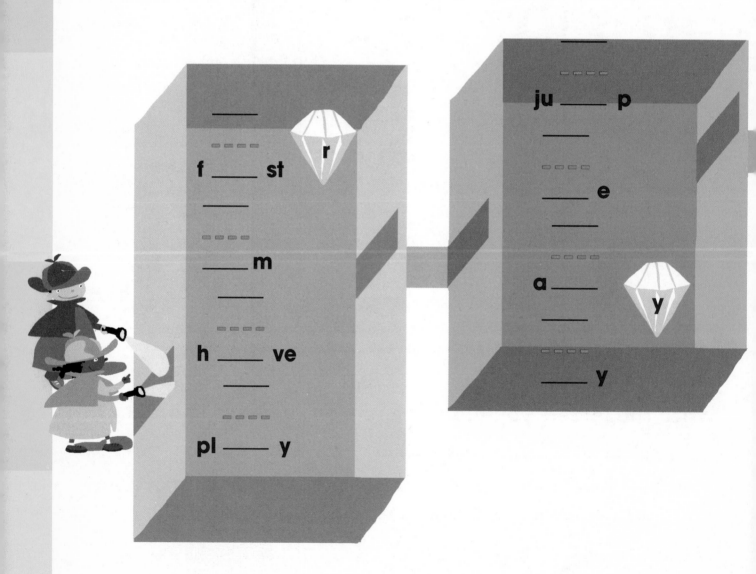

f ____ st

____ m

h ____ ve

pl ____ y

ju ____ p

____ e

a ____

____ y

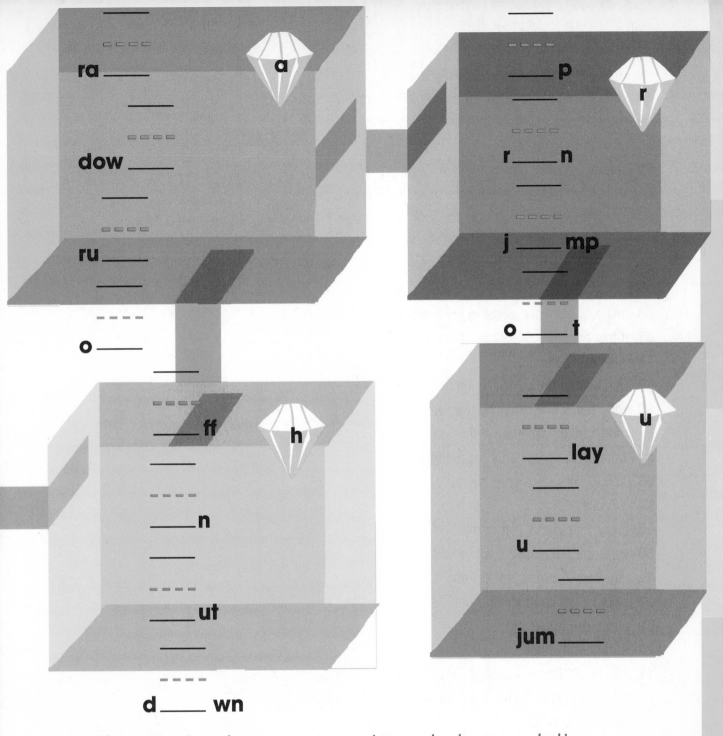

ra _____

dow _____

ru _____

o _____

_____ p

r _____ n

j _____ mp

o _____ t

_____ ff

_____ n

_____ ut

d _____ wn

_____ lay

u _____

jum _____

The missing letters are written below each line.
Look for the jewel that was found in the room
with that missing letter.
Write the letter from the jewel on the line.
The first one has been done for you.

___ ___ ___ ___ ___ ___ ___
h
___ ___ ___ ___ ___ ___ ___!
o p a u n m

Word Group 2 Answer Key

47 write I 4 times; names will vary

48 write I 5 times; numbers in boxes, left to right: 2; 5; 4; 1; 3

49 circle I 5 times; underline **am** 5 times

49 draw lines to match text to pictures

50 connect stars in I to **am** pattern

51 write **I am** 5 times; draw lines to match text to pictures

52 numbers in boxes, left to right: 1; 3; 4; 2; circle I 4 times; underline **have** 4 times

53 sneakers

54 write **am** 5 times; write **have** 5 times; name will vary

55 am, have; am, have; am, have; am, have

56 answers will vary; circle **my** 5 times

57 maze path should follow the word **my**

58 write **my** 7 times

59 numbers in boxes, left to right: 2; 1; 4 ; 3; circle I 4 times; draw a square around **me** 4 times

60 write **me** 5 times; he/she; answers will vary

61 match fruits; circle **my** 4 times; underline **me** 4 times

62 write **my** 5 times; write **me** 5 times

63 1. a; 2. am; 3. my; 4. me; a; am; my; me

64 a lizard

65 I; my; I; my; me; I; me; my

66 color these squares: I; me; my; I; me; me; I; I; my; me

67 numbers in boxes, left to right: 2; 3; 1; circle I 3 times; underline **run**, **play**, and **jump**

68 write I 3 times; underline **run**, **jump**, **play**; pictures should reflect action words in the sentence

69 jump; run; play

70 Run; Jump; Play

71 **Across:** 2. jump; 4. my; 5. have; **Down:** 1. run; 3. play; 4. me

72 run, ran; run, ran; run, ran; run, ran

73 write **ran** 5 times

74–75 write **fast** 7 times

76 up, down; up, down

77 left to right: on; in; on; on; in; in

78 out, in; in, out; in, out

79 on, off; on, off; on, off

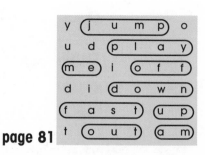

page 81

80 words with **m**: me, my; words with **o**: off, on, out; words with **r**: ran, run; words with **l/i**: I, in;

81 see right; hidden message: you did it!

82–83 fast, am, have, play; jump, me, am, my; ran, down, run, on;

up, run, jump, out; off, on, out, down; play, up, jump; hurray

I run. I jump. I am in!
My friends and I play,
play, play.

8

fold & assemble

Scholastic *100 Words Kids Need to Read by 1st Grade, Word Group 2*

1

Play, Play, Play
By Gail Tuchman
Illustrated by Greg Paprocki

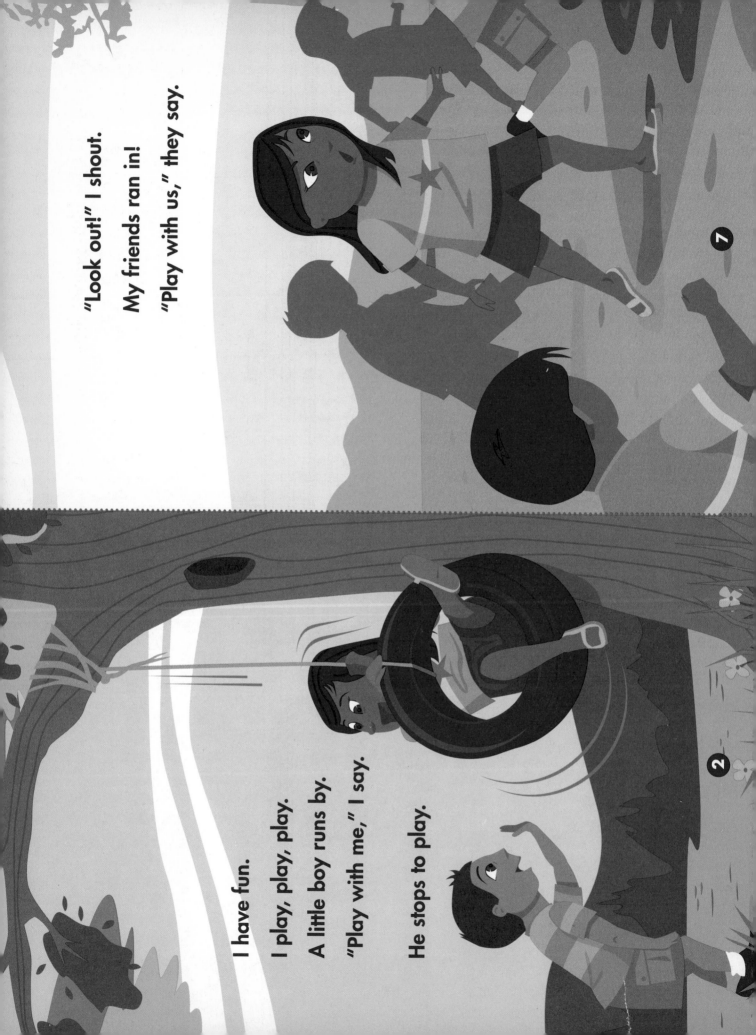

"Look out!" I shout.

My friends ran in!

"Play with us," they say.

7

I have fun.

I play, play, play.

A little boy runs by.

"Play with me," I say.

He stops to play.

2

I run up, down, in, and out.
My friends run up, down, in, and out.
I run fast. Run! Run! Run!
They run fast. Run! Run! Run!

6

I jump up.
The boy jumps up.
I jump down.
He jumps down.

3

More of my friends run by.

"Play with me," I say.

They stop to play.

I jump on and I jump off.

My friends jump on and off.

5

Two of my friends run by.

"Play with me," I say.

They stop to play.

I jump in and out.

The boy jumps in and out.

My friends jump in and out.

4

My Good Friend

Meet my good friend!

My good friend has a long tail.

My good friend has two floppy ears.

My good friend has black spots.

Circle the word (friend).
Underline the word **good**.

Who is your good friend?
Draw a picture of your friend
in the box.

Does your friend have floppy ears?
_____

- - - - - - - - - - - -

Write yes or no on the line. _____

Who Are Friends?

Draw a line to match the friends.

This is Dot.

Her friend has a hard shell.

"I am Harry's friend!"

"I am Sam's friend!"

This is Patsy.

Her friend has woolly fur.

"I am Dot's friend!"

This is Harry.

His friend says, "Moo!"

This is Sam.

His friend has a bushy tail.

"I am Patsy's friend!"

Who could be this animal's friend?
Draw its picture in the box.

Find a Friend

Write the missing letters to finish the word **friend**.

f r i e n ___

___ ___

f r i ___ n ___

f r ___ e ___ d

___ ___

___ ___ i e n d

___ ___ ___

f ___ ___ i ___ n d

___ ___ ___ ___

___ ___ ___ i e ___ ___ ___

May I Ask You a Question?

Reporters like to ask questions. You can be a reporter, too. Here are questions for you to ask. Complete each question by writing the word **you** on the line.

_____
- - - - - - - - - -
Who are _____ ?

_____
- - - - - - - - - -
When were _____ born?

_____
- - - - - - - - - -
Where were _____ born?

_____
- - - - - - - - - -
What do _____ like to do?

_____
- - - - - - - - - -
Which color do _____ like most?

_____
- - - - - - - - - -
Which food do _____ like most?

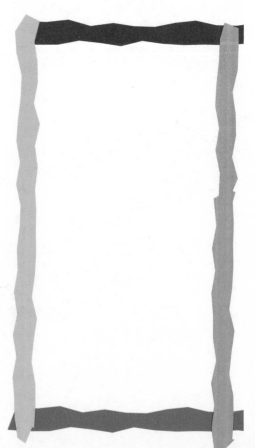

Ask a family member the questions above. Draw a picture of that person here. You could include his or her favorite food or color!

I Am Visiting You!

This space creature is coming to visit you!
First, draw a picture of you in the box.
Then draw a path from the space creature to you.
Follow the path that has the word **you** in it.

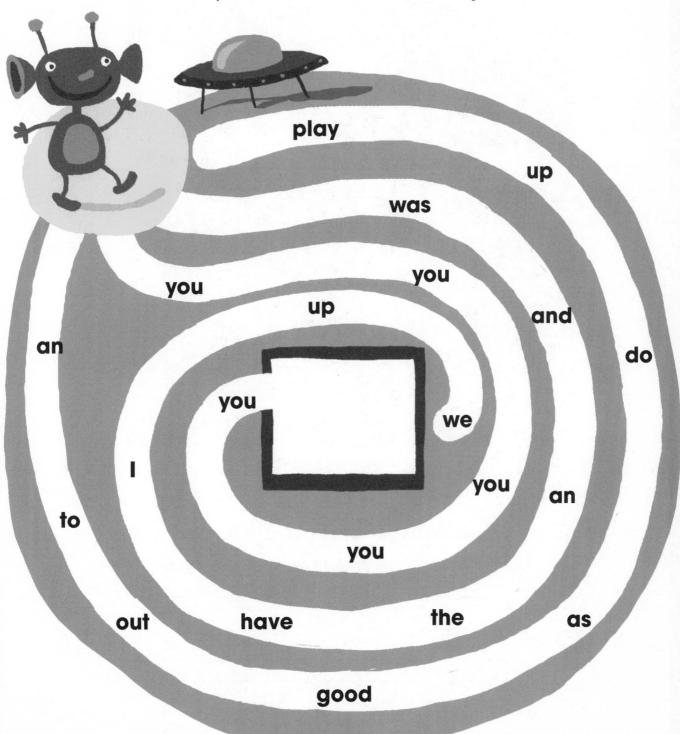

The Secret Square

What are these two monsters saying to each other? Solve the secret square to find out.

Write the circled letter on the first line. Count three squares. Circle the letter. Write the letter you circled on the next line. Keep going! Count three squares and write the letter to learn what the monsters are saying.

—— —— —— ——   —— —— —— ——

-- -- -- -- -- -- -- -- -- --   -- -- -- -- -- -- --

—— —— —— ——   —— —— —— ——

—— —— ——   —— —— —— —— —— —— ——

-- -- -- -- -- --   -- -- -- -- -- -- -- -- -- -- -- -- --

—— ——   —— —— —— —— —— ——

Monster Friends

One monster has written a letter to the other monster. The letter tells why they are friends. Write the word **are** on the lines to help the monster finish the letter.

I am glad you _____ my friend!

_____ You _____ nice.

You _____ always happy.

You _____ fun to be with.

You _____ a good monster friend.

You Are Good!

Color the spaces with the word **you** blue.
Color the spaces with the word **are** orange.
Color the spaces with the word **good** green.

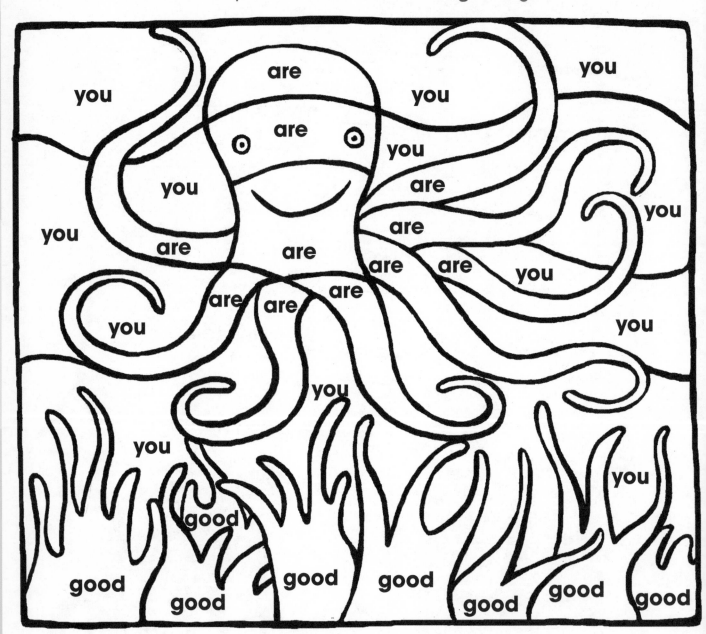

Which animal did you find?
Circle the name of the animal below.

fish   octopus   clam   shark

Go Fish

Look at all these fish. Circle the fish that have the word **and** in them.

Some of the fish with the word **and** also have a letter in them.

Write those letters here to tell what fish like to do:

___ ___ ___ ___

- - - - - - - - - - - - - - -

___ ___ ___ ___

Milk and Cookies

Read what these monsters like to eat. Use the words **and** or **good** to finish the sentences.

I like to eat milk _____ cookies.

They taste _____ .

I like to eat bananas _____ peanut butter.

They taste _____ .

I like to eat spinach _____ spaghetti.

They taste _____ .

I like to eat ice cream _____ mustard.

They taste _____ .

Draw foods you like to eat and finish the sentences.

I like to eat _____ .

They taste _____ .

More Fun Than One

It is easier to climb with a friend.
Color the rungs that have the word **we** to help
the two children climb to the top.

What Can We Make?

Write the word **and** on the line.

_____
- - - - - - - - - -

You _____ I = we!

Circle the word (and) in each sentence.
Write the word **We** on the line.

You and I get two sticks.

_____
- - - - - - - -

_____ get two sticks.

You and I tie the sticks together.

_____
- - - - - - - -

_____ tie the sticks together.

You and I cut the paper.

_____
- - - - - - - -

_____ cut the paper.

You and I tie the string.

_____
- - - - - - - -

_____ tie the string.

You and I add a tail.

_____
- - - - - - - -

_____ add a tail.

You and I fly a kite!

_____
- - - - - - - -

_____ fly a kite!

You or We?

Look at each picture. Circle the word that tells who is in the picture.

(You, We) read a book.

(You, We) ride a bike.

(You, We) play ball.

(You, We) play a game.

(You, We) eat a pizza.

I Can Do It!

Write the word **do** on the lines.

_____
- - - - - - - -

1. Who will milk the cow? I can _____ it!

_____
- - - - - - - -

2. Who will feed the chickens? I can _____ it!

_____
- - - - - - - -

3. Who will brush the horse? I can _____ it!

_____
- - - - - - - -

4. Who will pick the apples? I can _____ it!

Write the number of the sentence next to the correct child.

Do You Want To?

Write the words **Do** and **you** on the lines.
Then draw a line from the question to the
picture that shows the answer.

Yes, I do!

_____ _____

_____ _____ want to go to the beach?

Yes, I do!

_____ _____

_____ _____ want to color a picture?

Yes, I do!

_____ _____

_____ _____ want to bake cookies?

Yes, I do!

_____ _____

_____ _____ want to wash the dog?

Circle the word (Yes) in each answer.

Good Cat

Write the word **don't** on the line.

_____

do + not = -------------

_____

Write **Do not** or **Don't** to finish the sentences.

Do not eat the plant.

_____

_____ eat the plant.

_____ _____

_____ _____ chase the bird.

Don't chase the bird.

Do not scratch the couch.

_____

_____ scratch the couch.

What can you do?

You can hop up on my lap.

Good cat!

Rick and Nick

Help finish the story about Rick and Nick.
Write the word **don't** on the lines.

"I like these shoes,"
said Rick.

_____

- - - - - - - - - - -

"I _____," said Nick.

"They are too big."

"I like these shoes,"
said Rick.

_____

- - - - - - - - - - -

"I _____," said Nick.

"They are too high."

"I like these shoes,"
said Rick.

_____

- - - - - - - - - - -

"I _____," said Nick.

"They are too crazy."

"I like these shoes,"
said Rick.

_____

- - - - - - - - - - -

"I _____," said Nick.

"They are too long."

"What shoes *do* you like?"
asked Rick.

"I like these shoes," said Nick.

"They are the ones on my feet!"

Do or Don't?

Put an X in the box to answer
each question.

Do cats like to take a bath?   ☐ do   ☐ don't

Do you like to take a bath?   ☐ do   ☐ don't

Do fish have fur?   ☐ do   ☐ don't

Do bears have fur?   ☐ do   ☐ don't

Do acorns grow into oak trees?   ☐ do   ☐ don't

Do chicks grow into chickens?   ☐ do   ☐ don't

Do birds like to sing?   ☐ do   ☐ don't

Do you like to sing?   ☐ do   ☐ don't

Do Go the Right Way!

Help the explorer reach the statue. Color the stones that have the word **do**. This secret passageway has many traps. Don't fall into them!

do	do	don't	don't	don't	don't
don't	do	don't	don't	don't	don't
don't	do	do	don't	don't	don't
don't	don't	do	do	do	don't
don't	don't	don't	don't	do	do

Yes or No?

Look at each picture. Read the question.
Write **yes** or **no** to answer the question.

Do you see a bird? _____

Do you see a rock? _____

Do you see a flower? _____

Do you see a fish? _____

Do you see a turtle? _____

Do you see a bus? _____

Fair Fun

Circle the word **yes** or **no** in each sentence.

Then write the word **do** or **don't** on the line.

Do you want to go to the fair?

_____

Yes! I_____.

Do you want to play a game?

_____

Yes! I_____.

Do you want to go on the roller coaster?

_____

Yes! I_____.

Do you want cotton candy?

_____

No! I_____.

Do you want to go on the Ferris wheel?

_____

No! I_____.

Do you want some lemonade?

_____

No! I_____.

Word Maker

Follow the directions to make new words.

1. Write the word **you.**

_____

- - - - - - - - - - - -

_____

2. Change the **y** to a **d** and take off the **u.**

_____

- - - - - - - - - -

_____

3. Change the **d** to an **n.**

_____

- - - - - - - - - - -

_____

4. Add the letter **t** to the end.

_____

- - - - - - - - - - -

_____

Use the words you wrote to complete these sentences. Hint: You may have to use a capital letter.

_____

- - - - - - - - - - - -

" _____ and I are good friends," said the cat.

_____

- - - - - - - - - - - -

" _____ you know why?"

_____

- - - - - - - - - -

" _____ ," said the dog. "Tell me."

_____

- - - - - - - - - - -

"We are _____ alike," said the cat.

"But we do like the same thing—naps!"

No, It Is Not!

Is it a zebra?

Read the question. Look at the picture.
Write the words **No** and **not** on the lines.

_____ _____
- - - - - - -   - - - - - - - -
_____ , it is _____ .

Is it a kangaroo?

Is it an elephant?

_____ _____
- - - - - - -   - - - - - - - -
_____ , it is _____ .

_____ _____
- - - - - - -   - - - - - - - - -
_____ , it is _____ .

Is it a hippo?

Circle the animal word in
each question and draw a
line to its correct picture.

_____ _____
- - - - - - -   - - - - - - - -
_____ , it is _____ .

Seashells

Collect the seashells!
Circle the shells that have
the word **not** in them.

not
b

not
c

yes
s

do
k

no
d

not
h

don't
m

not
e

not
a

you
i

Each shell also has one extra letter in it.
Write the letters from the shells with the word **not** here:

——— ——— ——— ——— ———

- - - - - - - - - - - - - - - - - -

——— ——— ——— ——— ——— .

Now unscramble the letters to find a word
that completes the sentence.

You can find seashells at the

——— ——— ——— ——— ———

- - - - - - - - - - - - - - - - - -

——— ——— ——— ——— ——— .

I Did My Chores

Help Danny go out to play.
First, circle the word (did) in the question.
Then write the word **did** on the line.

Did you make your bed?   Yes, I _____ .

Did you feed the dog?   Yes, I _____ .

Did you water the plants? Yes, I _____ .

Did you do your homework? Yes, I _____ .

Okay! You can go outside!

Party Checklist

The monsters are having a party!
Read the checklist.

For the items with a ✔,
write the word **did** on the line.

For the items without a ✔,
write the words **did not** on the line.

_____
- - - - - - - - -

✔ Send invitations. _____

_____
- - - - - - - - -

✔ Make mud punch. _____

_____ _____
- - - - - - - - - - - - - - - - -

Bake lizard pie. _____ _____

_____
- - - - - - - - -

✔ Order awful band music. _____

_____
- - - - - - - - -

Set up pin-the-tale-on-the-monster game. _____

Here They Come!

The monsters are coming to the party.
Circle the word (they) in the sentences.

1. Here they come!

   They are bringing presents.

2. Here they come!

   They are bringing hats.

3. Here they come!

   They are bringing frogs.

4. Here they come!

   They are bringing pizza.

Match the sentences with the monsters
in the picture. Write the number of the
sentence next to the correct monsters.

Going to the City

We are going to the city.	They are going to the city, too.
We are going to the library.	They are going to the library, too.
We are going to a play.	They are going to a play, too.
We are going to the zoo.	They are going to the zoo, too.

Circle the word **We**.
Draw a square around the word **They**.
Underline the word **are**.

The Baseball Game

Write the word **They** on the lines
to replace the blue words in each sentence.

The baseball players ran onto the field.
_____

- - - - - - - - - - - - - -

_____ ran onto the field.

The people cheered and clapped.
_____

- - - - - - - - - - - - - -

_____ cheered and clapped.

The pitchers threw balls to the batters.
_____

- - - - - - - - - - - - - -

_____ threw the ball to the batters.

The runners ran around the bases.
_____

- - - - - - - - - - - - - -

_____ ran around the bases.

Both teams had fun at the game.
_____

- - - - - - - - - - - - - -

_____ had fun at the game.

Mothers and Fathers

Who do you see in these pictures?
Write the word **mother** or **father**
to tell who you see with each child.

My Mother and Father

Write **mother**, **father**, or **they** on the lines.

_____

My _____ and father play games with me.

_____ play games with me.

_____

My mother and _____ help me.

_____ help me.

My mother and father are great!

_____ are great.

Put a ⭐
above the word **mother**.

Put a ♡
above the word **father**.

My mother and father teach me new things.

_____ teach me new things.

_____   _____

My _____ and _____ love me!

_____ love me.

Finding Opposites

Read each word. Find the opposite word in the box. Write that word on the line.

Word Box

don't	father	no	they	you

do ___ ___ ___ , ___   I ___ ___ ___
    7   2   8   3

mother ___ ___ ___ ___ ___ ___
      4   10 5

we ___ ___ ___ ___   yes ___ ___
    6 1   9

Write the numbered letters on the lines to reveal a secret message.

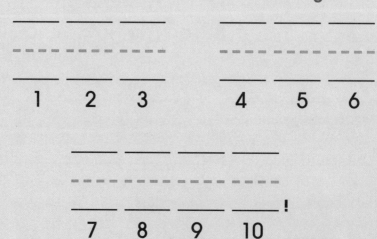

___ ___ ___   ___ ___ ___
 1   2   3   4   5   6

___ ___ ___ ___ !
 7   8   9 10

I Had
Draw a line to match the pictures.

I have an apple.

I had a banana.

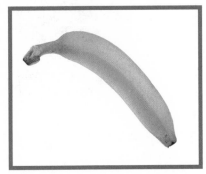

I have a banana.

I had an apple.

I have grapes.

I had a peach

I have a peach.

I had grapes.

Circle the word (have). Underline the word **had**.

I Had Poem

Finish the poem. Write the word **had** on each line.

_____

- - - - - - - - - - -

I _____ a pickle.

It was pretty thick.

_____

- - - - - - - - - - -

I _____ a sticker.

It would not stick.

_____

- - - - - - - - - - -

I _____ a penny.

I gave it to you.

_____

- - - - - - - - - - -

I _____ a mitten.

I lost it, too.

_____

- - - - - - - - - - -

I _____ a ball.

It rolled away.

I have a puppy!

It is here to stay.

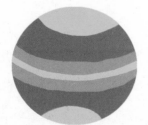

Where Were You?

Write the word **were** on the lines.

3. Where _____ you?

We _____ in the deli.

1. Where _____ you?

We _____ in the flower shop.

4. Where _____ you?

We _____ in the bike shop.

2. Where _____ you?

We _____ in the hardware store.

Write the number of the sentence next to the correct picture.

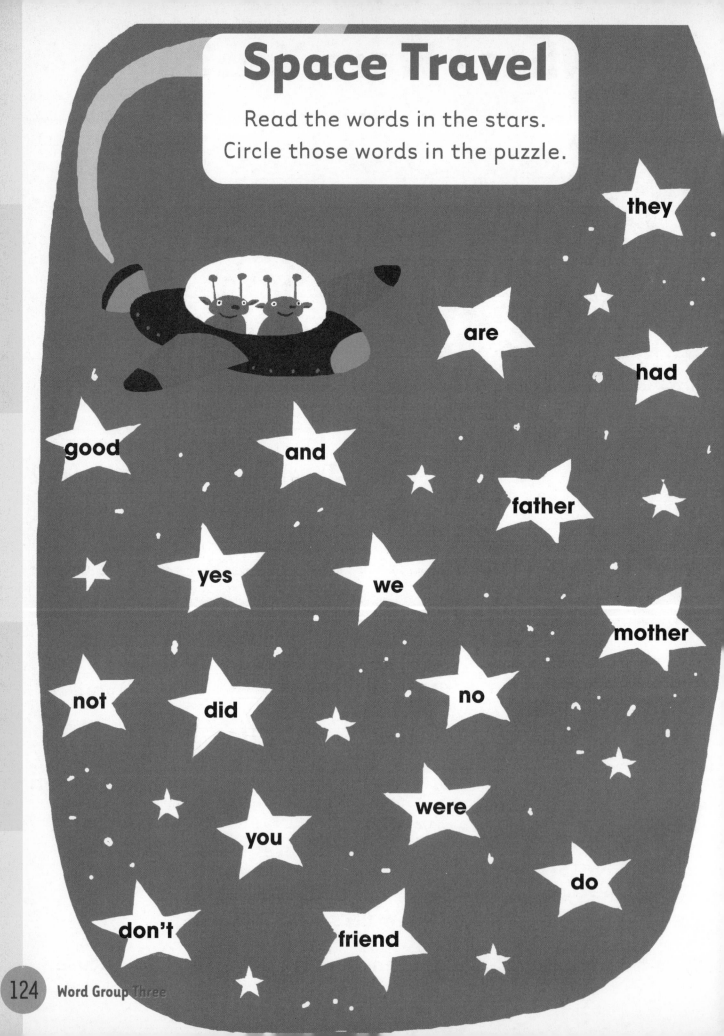

Space Travel

Read the words in the stars.
Circle those words in the puzzle.

they

are

had

good

and

father

yes

we

mother

not

did

no

were

you

do

don't

friend

w f r i e n d e
w e r e l y o u
d i d n o t w e
c o m o t h e r
a n d m y e s e
t f a t h e r o
h a d p d o n t
l a a r e n d o
g o o d e t n o
s p t h e y o t

Read the message from the space creatures! Write the letters you **didn't** circle in order on the lines below.

_____

\- \- \- \- \- \- \- \- \- \- \- \- \- \- \- \- \- \-

_____

___ _____

\- \- \- \- \- \- \- \- \- \- \- \- \- \- \- \-

___ _____

_____

\- \- \- \- \- \- \- \- \- \- \- \-

_____!

89 circle **friend** 4 times; underline **good** 4 times

90 line should match: duck to turtle; pig to sheep; horse to cow; snake to squirrel

91 complete **friend** 6 times

92 write **you** 6 times

93 correct maze path follows **you**

94 you are my friend

95 write **are** 5 times

96 octopus is orange; seaweed is green; water is blue; octopus

97 circle 5 fish; swim

98 write **and** 5 times; write **good** 5 times

99 color 7 jungle gym bars with **we**

100 and; circle **and** 6 times; write **we** 6 times

101 left to right: you; you; we; we; we

102 write **do** 4 times; numbers from left to right: 1; 3; 2; 4

103 write **Do you** 4 times; circle **Yes** 4 times; draw lines to match text to photos

104 write Don't; Do not; Don't

105 write **don't** 4 times

106 do, answers will vary; don't, do; do, do; do, answers will vary

107 10 stones should be colored

108 no; no; yes; yes; no; yes

109 do; do; do; don't; don't; don't

110 1. you; 2. do; 3. no; 4. not; You; Do; No; not

111 write **no** 4 times; write **not** 4 times; circle the words zebra, hippo, kangaroo, elephant and draw lines from circled words to correct photos

112 circle 5 seashells with **not**; beach

113 circle the word **did** 4 times

114 did; did; did not; did; did not

115 circle **They** 8 times; numbers from left to right: 1; 3; 2; 4

116 circle **we** 4 times; draw a square around **they** 4 times; underline **are** 8 times

117 write **they** 5 times

118 father; mother; mother; father; mother

119 mother, they; father, they; they; they; mother, father, they; draw stars above **mother** 5 times; draw hearts above **father** 5 times

120 don't; you; father; they; no; you are done

121 circle **have** 4 times; underline **had** 4 times; draw lines to match apple & core; banana & peel; grapes & stems; peach & pit

122 write **had** 5 times

123 write **were** 8 times; numbers from left to right: 1; 3; 2; 4

124–125 see right; WELCOME TO PLANET SPOT!

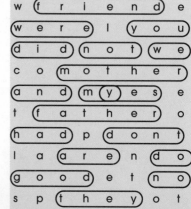

page 125

Max and Dan were hungry.

"Do you see my mother?" said Max.

"No. I don't see her," said Dan.

"Do you see my father?" said Max.

"No. I don't see him," said Dan.

"Uh-oh," said Max.

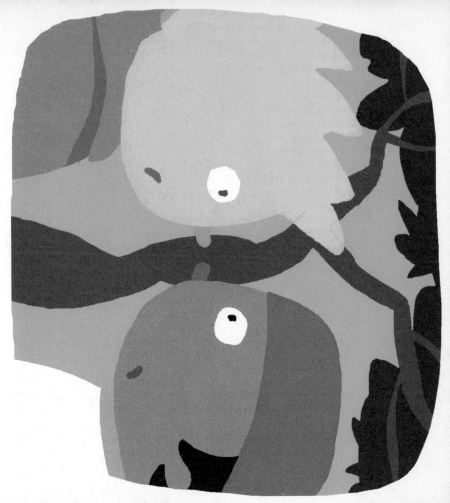

One day Max and Dan went to the zoo.

They saw lions.

The lions were big.

They had big teeth.

Next the two friends saw bears.

One bear growled at Max.

"Did he scare you?" said Dan.

"No. Bears don't scare me," said Max.

"Are you scared?" Max asked Dan.

"No," said Dan.

"Those lions do not scare me."

Hello, Good Day!

Circle the word (day) in each sentence.

"Hello!" said the squirrel.

"Good day!" said the rabbit.

"It is a nice day," said the squirrel.

"A great day!" said the rabbit.

"Have a good day," said the squirrel.

"Have a good day!" said the rabbit.

Write the word **day** on the lines below. Draw a picture of the rabbit's new friend in the box.

_____

"Good _____ !" said the rabbit.

_____

"Good _____ !" said the turtle.

Weather Words

Write the word **day** on the lines
Draw the type of day in the box.

_____ - - - - - - - It is a cloudy _____ .	_____ - - - - - - - It is a sunny _____ .
_____ - - - - - - - It is a rainy _____ .	_____ - - - - - - - It is a snowy _____ .

Day and Night

It is day!

The sun shines during the day.

Birds chirp during the day.

We go to school during the day.

It is night!

The moon shines at night.

The owl hoots at night.

We go to sleep at night.

Draw a sun around the word **day**.
Draw a moon around the word **night**.

Night Animal

Color the spaces with the word **night** brown.

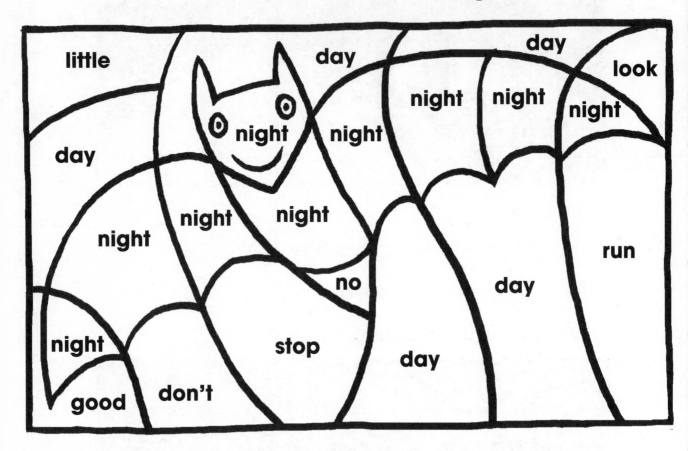

Write the word **night** on the lines.

_____

Bats come out of their caves at _____ .

_____

Bats fly at _____ .

_____

Some bats eat berries at _____ .

_____

You might see bats in the sky at _____ .

If You See . . .

Circle the word (if) in each sentence.
Write **day** or **night** to complete
each sentence.

If you see the moon,

_____

- - - - - - - - - - - - - - - - -

it is _____ .

If you see the sun,

_____

- - - - - - - - - -

it is _____ .

If you see the stars,

_____

- - - - - - - - - - - - - - - - - -

it is _____ .

If you see your shadow,

_____

- - - - - - - - - - - -

it is _____ .

Draw a line to match
the sentence to the picture.

What If?

Write the word **if** on each line. Then draw yourself in the picture frames.

What _____ you were an astronaut?

Draw yourself here.

What _____ you were a firefighter?

You would have a hot job!

What _____ you drove an ice cream truck?

You would have a cool job!

What _____ you were an explorer?

Draw yourself here!

What _____ you were in a monster movie?

Draw yourself here!

Missing Letters

The monsters wrote the words **day**, **night**, and **if**, but they forgot some letters. Write in the missing letters.

____
- - -
____ i g h t

____
- - -
n ____ g h t

__
- - -
i ____

____
- - -
n i g h ____

____
- - -
d a ____

If I Find the Treasure . . .

Help the sailor find the buried treasure.
Trace the path that has the word **if**.

as · if · a

up

on · if

at

if

will

is

if

be

for

I

if

of

it · if · did

if · if

Look! A Planet!

Circle the stars that have the word **look**.

look

look

done

not

look

look

stop

look

don't

to

look

boy

Look! I See . . .

Write the word **Look** on each line. Circle the word (a).

_____

- - - - - - - - - -

1. _____! I see a butterfly.   _____

_____

- - - - - - - - - -

2. _____! I see a bird.

- - - - - - - - - -

3. _____! I see a skunk.

_____

- - - - - - - - - -

4. _____! I see a chipmunk.

Write the number of the sentence next to the correct animal in the picture.

Look at That!

Write the word **Look** on the line. Color the animals.

_____

- - - - - - - - - - -

_____at the lizard!

It is **green**.

_____

- - - - - - - - -

_____ at the ladybug!

It is **red** and **black**.

_____

- - - - - - - - -

_____ at the bear!

It is **brown**.

_____

- - - - - - - - -

_____ at the bird!

It is **blue**.

Look Out!

Help the boy snowboard down the hill.
First, color in the trees with the words **Look out!**

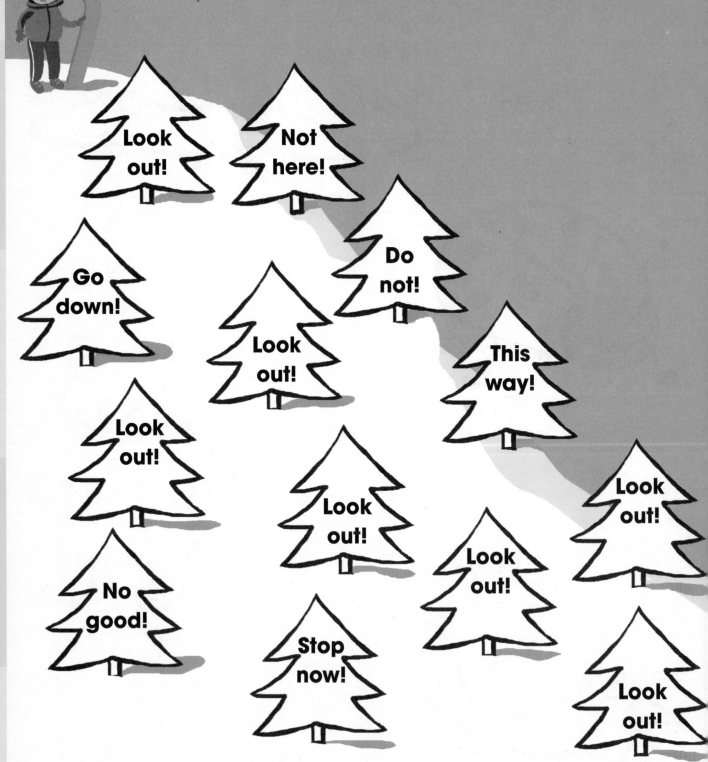

Look out!

Not here!

Go down!

Do not!

Look out!

This way!

Look out!

Look out!

Look out!

No good!

Look out!

Stop now!

Look out!

Look out!

Now trace a path between the trees you colored in.

The Busy Day

Yesterday, I was busy!

I went to school.

I went to the park.

I went to the store.

I went to the movies.

I went to bed.

Circle the word (went) in the sentences.

Where did you go yesterday?

Draw a picture of that place.
Then finish the sentence.

I went to the _____ .

Where Did You Go?

Circle the word (go) in the first sentence.
Write the word **went** on the line.

_____

- - - - - - - - - - -

Where did you go? I _____ to the pet shop.

_____

- - - - - - - - - - -

Where did you go? I _____ to the hat shop.

_____

- - - - - - - - - - -

Where did you go? I _____ to the doughnut shop.

_____

- - - - - - - - - - -

Where did you go? I _____ to the skateboard shop.

_____

- - - - - - - - - - -

Where did you go? I _____ to the flower shop.

Explore a Cave

Help these people explore the big cave.
Put an X on the tunnels that have the word **Stop**!
These caves do not go anywhere.

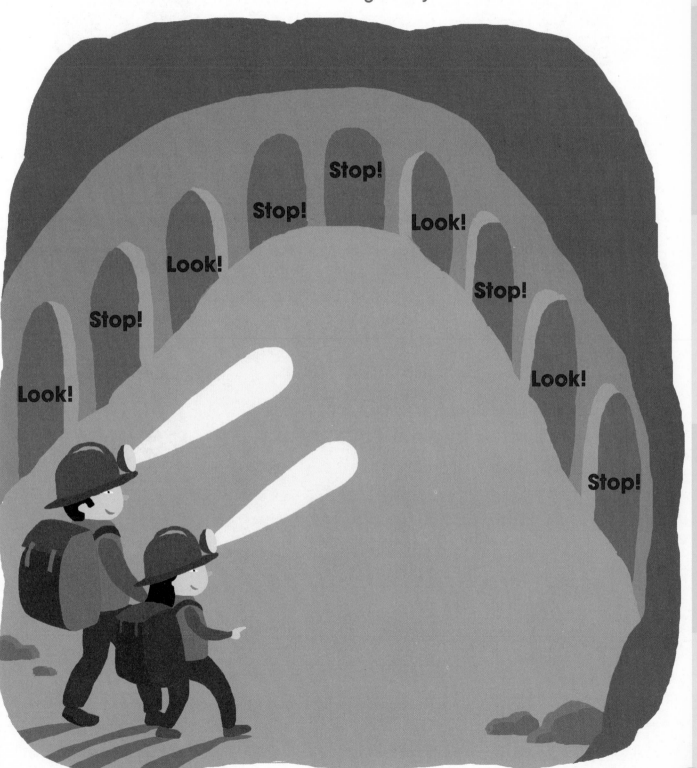

Stop and Look

Write the word **stop** below the signs. Write the word **look** below the pictures.

_____

- - - - - - - - -

_____

- - - - - - - - -

_____

_____

- - - - - - - - -

_____

- - - - - - - - -

_____

_____

- - - - - - - - -

_____

- - - - - - - - -

_____

_____

- - - - - - - - -

_____

- - - - - - - - -

_____

Draw a line to match the sign with the picture.

Puzzle Pieces

Combine the puzzle pieces to make a word.
Write the word on the line.

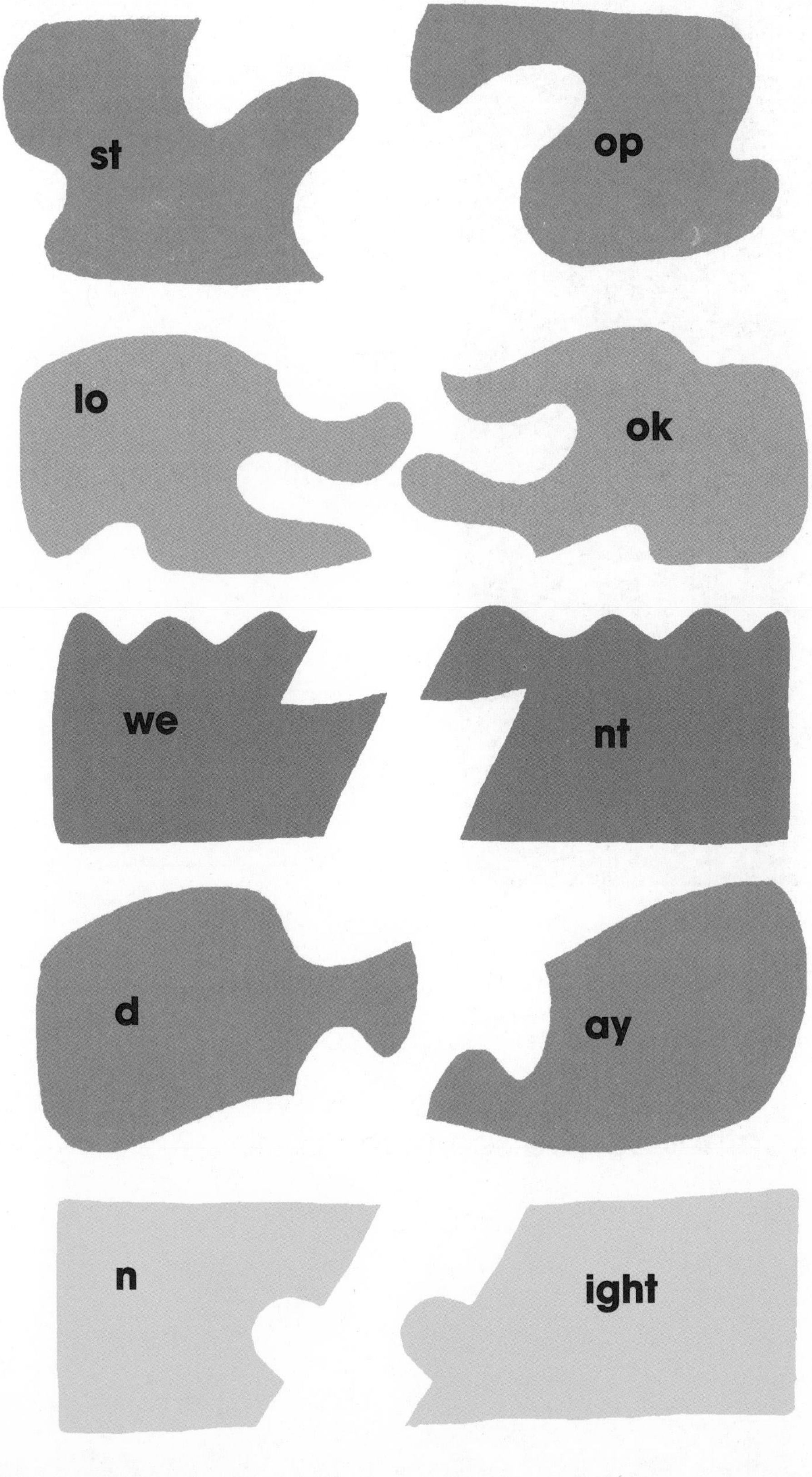

st op

_____

lo ok

_____

we nt

_____

d ay

_____

n ight

_____

Rain

Rain falling on my feet.

Rain falling on the street.

Rain falling on my face.

Rain falling every place!

Circle the word (rain) in the poem.
Then answer this question:

What weather do you see in the picture?

_____

- -

_____

Rain or Shine

When the sun shines,

you can . . .

play ball.

skip rope.

play with friends.

Circle the word **rain**. Write the word **rain** on the line.

When the rain falls, you can . . .

get wet.

splash in puddles.

play with friends.

_____

When the _____ falls, I can . . .

Draw a picture
of yourself in
the rain.

Rain Gear

Color the spaces with the word **rain** yellow.
Color the spaces with the word **look** blue.
Color the spaces with the word **stop** gray.

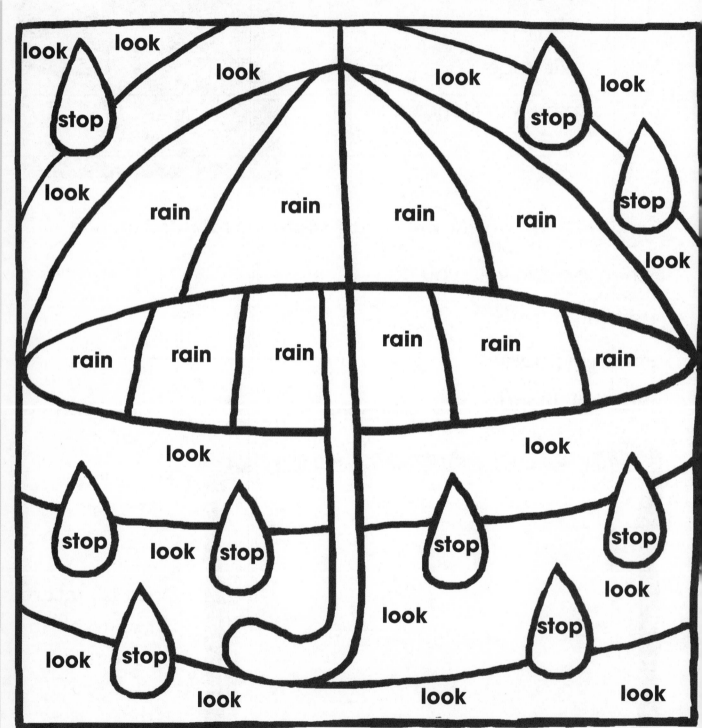

Happy Birthday!

Tomorrow is my birthday!

I will play games.

I will see friends.

I will eat ice cream.

I will have a cake.

I will blow out the candles.

I will get presents.

I will say, "Thank you!"

Circle the word will in the sentences. What will you do on your birthday? Draw a picture of it in the box.

School Time

Write the word **will** on the lines.

I am going to school.

_____

I _____ add math problems.

_____

_____   I _____ read stories.

I _____ do science experiments.

_____

I _____ play with my friends.

Write the word **will** under the pictures that show things described in the sentences above.

_____   _____   _____

What Will It Be?

Draw a line to match the baby animal
with the adult animal.

Someday, a kitten will be a

chicken.

Someday, a chick will be a

dog.

Someday, a puppy will be a

butterfly.

Someday, a caterpillar will be a

cat.

Underline the word **will**. Circle the word (be).

Be Careful!

Show the diver how to reach the ship.
Color the squares with the word **be**.

be	by	boy	I	at
be	be	he	she	to
by	be	I	the	was
boy	be	be	be	by
on	you	if	be	do
he	by	the	be	be

Word Whiz

Make words by following the directions.

1. Write the word **me**.

2. Change the **e** to a **y**.

3. Change the **m** to a **b**.

4. Change the **y** to an **e**.

Now use the words you wrote to finish the story.

This is a story about _____ .

This is _____ puppy Rex.

He likes to sit _____ me.

One day, Rex will _____ a dog!

Rex will always _____ _____ dog.

Don't Sit There!

Write the word **sit** on the lines.

_____
- - - - - - - - - -
1. Don't _____ on the ☘ !

_____
- - - - - - - - - -
2. Don't _____ on the 🍕 !

_____
- - - - - - - - - -
3. Don't_____ on the 🪣 !

_____
- - - - - - - - - -
4. Don't _____ on the 🐱 !

Write the number of the sentence
next to the correct monster in the picture.

The Cat Sat

Write the word **sat** on the lines.

Yesterday

_____

- - - - - - - - - - - - -

The cat _____ on the sofa.

_____

- - - - - - - - - - - - -

The cat _____ on the chair.

_____

- - - - - - - - - - - - -

The cat _____ on the table.

_____

- - - - - - - - - - - - -

The cat _____ on my hair!

Write the word **sit** on the lines.

Today

_____

- - - - - - - - - - - - -

The cats _____ on the counter.

_____

- - - - - - - - - - - - -

The cats _____ in the shoe.

_____

- - - - - - - - - - - - -

The cats _____ in the basket.

_____

- - - - - - - - - - - - -

The cats _____ on you!

Sit and Sat

Write the word **sit** or **sat**
to finish the sentence.

_____

- - - - - - - - - - -

Where did you_____?

_____

- - - - - - - - - -

I _____on the chair.

_____

- - - - - - - - - -

Where did you_____?

_____

- - - - - - - - -

I _____on the chair.

_____

- - - - - - - - - -

Where did you_____?

_____

- - - - - - - - -

I _____in the tree!

_____

- - - - - - - - - -

Where did you_____?

_____

- - - - - - - - -

I _____on the bench.

What Do You Eat?

Write the word **eat** to finish the questions.

_____

What can you _____ for breakfast?

Circle that food in the picture.

_____

What do you _____ for lunch?

Underline that food in the picture.

_____

What can you _____ for a snack?

Draw a square around that food in the picture.

_____

What can you _____ for dinner?

Put a check by that food in the picture.

I Ate Too Much!

Complete the story by writing the word **ate** on the lines.

_____

- - - - - - - - - -

Yesterday I went to a party. I _____ too much!

_____

- - - - - - - - - -

They had ice cream. I _____ too much!

_____

- - - - - - - - - -

They had cake. I _____ too much!

_____

- - - - - - - - - -

They had pizza. I _____ too much!

_____

- - - - - - - - - -

They had tacos. I _____ too much!

Circle the right word.

Next time I got to a party, I won't (eat, ate) so much!

What's for Lunch?

Circle the correct word for each sentence.

Yesterday, I (eat, ate) a sandwich.   Yesterday, I (eat, ate) a cookie.

Today, I will (eat, ate) some soup.   Today, I will (eat, ate) a cracker.

Yesterday, I (eat, ate) an apple.

Today, I will (eat, ate) a banana.

Yesterday, I (eat, ate) a carrot.

Today, I will (eat, ate) some celery.

For You!

Write the word **for** in the sentences. Then draw a line from the sentence to the correct picture.

_____
- - - - - - -
These shoes are_____ a gardener.

_____
- - - - - - -
These shoes are _____ a clown.

_____
- - - - - - -
These shoes are _____ a dancer.

_____
- - - - - - -
These boots are _____ a firefighter.

_____
- - - - - - -
These shoes are _____ a runner.

Draw a picture of some wild shoes and write the word **for**.

_____
- - - - - - -
These shoes are _____ fun!

Who Is It From?

Circle the word (for). Write the word **from** to finish the sentence.

This hat is for you.

_____

- - - - - - - - - - - - -

It is _____ Aunt Pearl.

This shirt is for you.

_____

- - - - - - - - - - - - -

It is _____ Uncle Bob.

This scarf is for you.

_____

- - - - - - - - - - - - -

It is _____ Grandpa Jones.

These shoes are for you.

_____

- - - - - - - - - - - - -

They are _____ Grandma Rose.

Now you are dressed up!

Pig Tales

Write the word **of** on the lines to finish the story.

This is the story _____ the three little pigs.

One pig built a house _____ straw.

The big, bad wolf blew it down.

One pig built a house _____ sticks.

The big, bad wolf blew it down.

One pig built a house _____ bricks.

The big, bad wolf huffed and puffed.

He could not blow the brick house down.

And inside _____ it, sat three smart pigs!

Who Do You Play With?

Write the word **with** to finish each sentence.

I read _____ my sister.

I sing _____ my bird.

I play _____ my friend.

I sleep _____ my bear.

Write the word **with** on the line.
Draw a picture in the box to
complete the sentence.

I play _____ my _____.

Raise a Flag

Help raise the flags on the castle!
Read the words in each flag.

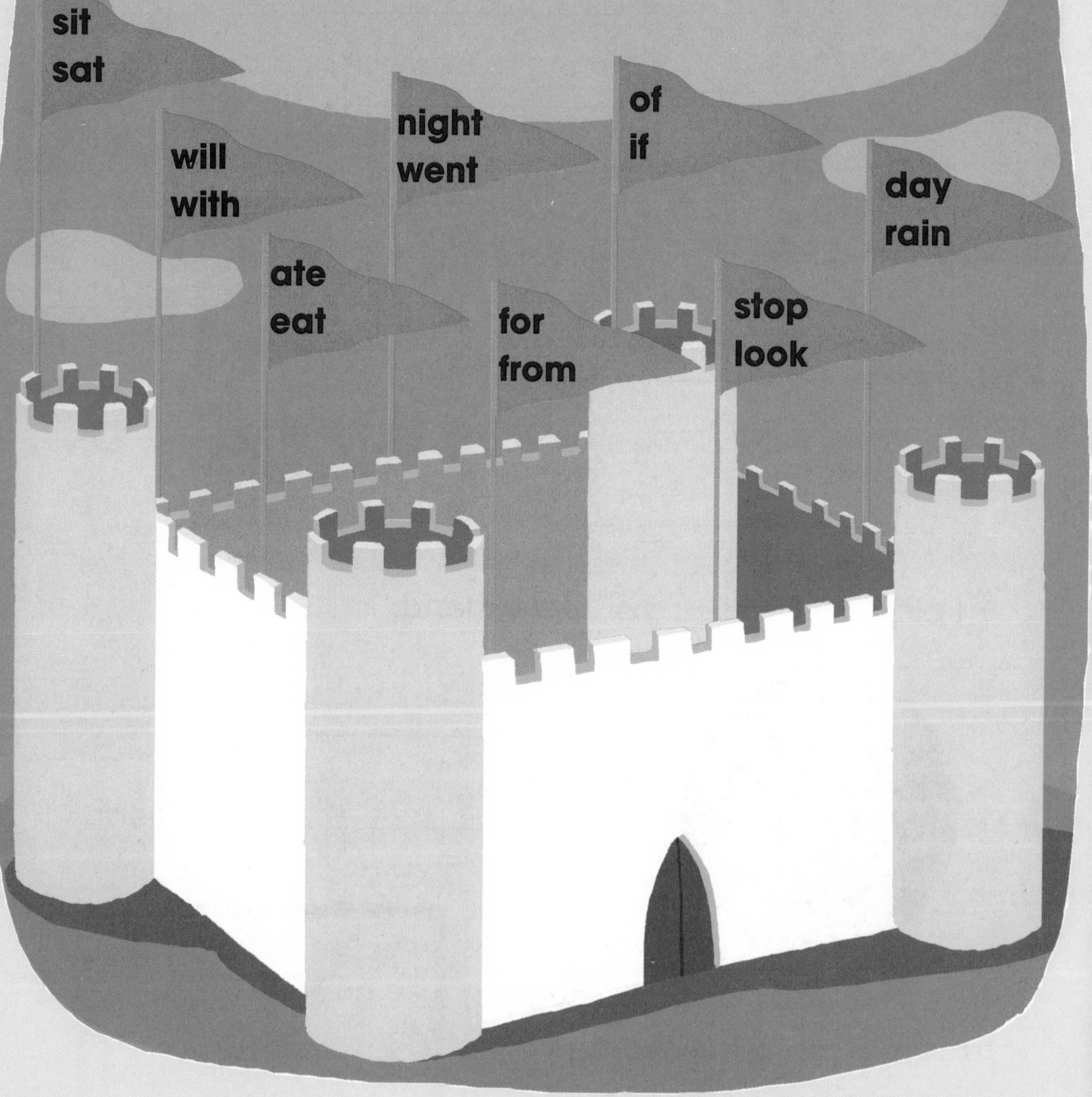

sit
sat

will
with

night
went

of
if

day
rain

ate
eat

for
from

stop
look

1. Words with w or i.

_____   _____   _____

_____   _____   _____

_____   _____   _____

Read the clues.
Write three words that fit each clue on the lines.

2. Words with **o**.

_____ _____ _____

---------------------- ---------------------- ----------------------

_____ _____ _____

3. Words with **r**.

_____ _____ _____

---------------------- ---------------------- ----------------------

_____ _____ _____

4. Words with **f**.

_____ _____ _____

---------------------- ---------------------- ----------------------

_____ _____ _____

5. Words with **a**.

_____ _____ _____

---------------------- ---------------------- ----------------------

_____ _____ _____

6. Words with **s** or **t**.

_____ _____ _____

---------------------- ---------------------- ----------------------

_____ _____ _____

7. Words with **n** or **t**.

_____ _____ _____

---------------------- ---------------------- ----------------------

_____ _____ _____

Word Group 4 Answer Key

131 circle **day** 5 times; write **day** 2 times; drawing should be of a turtle

132 write **day** 4 times

133 draw a sun around **day** 4 times; draw a moon around **night** 4 times

134 a bat; write **night** 4 times

135 circle **if** 4 times; night; day; night; day; match photos to sentences

136 write **if** 5 times

137 n; i; f; t; y

138 correct maze path follows **if**

139 circle 6 stars

140 write **look** 4 times; circle **a** 4 times; left to right: 3; 1; 4; 2

141 write **look** 4 times; color pictures as noted

142 color 6 trees

143 circle **went** 5 times; answers will vary

144 circle **go** 5 times; write **went** 5 times

145 Put an X on the 5 cave mouths with **stop**

146 write **stop** 4 times; write **look** 4 times; draw lines to match signs and pictures

147 stop; look; went; day; night

148 circle **rain** 4 times; rain

149 circle **rain** 1 time; rain

150 umbrella

151 circle **will** 7 times

152 write **will** 4 times; write **will** under the 1st and 3rd pictures

153 draw lines to match kitten & cat; chick & chicken; puppy & dog; caterpillar & butterfly; underline **will** 4 times; circle **be** 4 times

154 color 10 squares with **be**

155 me; my; by; be; me; my; by; be; be; my

156 write **sit** 4 times; numbers from left to right: 1; 4; 3; 2

157 write **sat** 4 times; write **sit** 4 times

158 write **sit**, **sat** 4 times

159 write **eat** 4 times; answers will vary

160 write **ate** 5 times; eat

161 ate, eat; ate, eat; ate, eat; ate, eat

162 write **for** 5 times; match pictures to sentences; for

163 circle **for** 4 times; write **from** 4 times

164 write **of** 5 times

165 write **with** 4 times; with

166–167 answers will vary among: 1. will, with, sit, night, if, rain, went; 2. for, from, of, stop, look; 3. for, from, rain; 4. from, for, if, of; 5. ate, sat, eat, day, rain; 6. sit, ate, eat, stop; 7. sit, ate, night, sat, with, eat, went, stop, rain

I went to play with my pup.
My pup plays with a box of balls.
"Be good," I say. "Be good."
My pup will not be good.

"Look!" I say. "This is for you."
"You can eat it if you sit.
My pup looked at me.
He sat and ate.

"Look!" I say. "This is for you."

"You can eat it if you stop."

My pup looked at me.

He stopped and ate.

5

I went for a run with my pup.

My pup runs fast.

"Stop," I say. "Stop. Stop."

My pup will not stop.

4

Can You Read It?

Help the detective read the secret message.
Find the books with the word **can** on the cover. Circle them.

Write the letters for each book
you circled in order on the lines below.

—— —— —— —— —— —— —— ——

Adding Letters

Make new words by following the directions.

```
____
```

1. Write the word **a**.

```
____
```

```
_____
```

2. Add the letter **n** to the end.

```
_____
```

```
_____
```

3. Add the letter **c** to the beginning.

```
_____
```

Write the word **can** on the lines.
Then draw a line to match the
sentences with the animals in the picture.

A bird _____ fly.

A fish _____ swim.

A duck _____ float.

A frog _____ hop.

A dog _____ bark.

Can You?

Write the word **can** to finish the sentences. Circle the word (Can) in the questions.

_____

- - - - - - - - - -

I _____ climb.

Can you climb?

_____

- - - - - - - - - -

I _____ hop.

Can you hop?

_____

- - - - - - - - - -

I _____ swing.

Can you swing?

_____

- - - - - - - - - -

I _____ run.

Can you run?

Draw a picture of yourself in the box doing one of the animal actions. Then finish the sentence.

_____ _____

- - - - - - - - - - - - - - - - - -

I _____ _____ .

Paper Fun

Write the word **can** on the line. Then draw a line to match the sentence with the picture.

_____

I _____ make an airplane.

_____

I _____ make a flower.

_____

I _____ make a hat.

_____

I _____ make a boat.

_____

I _____ make a bird.

I See You!

Write the word **see** on the lines.

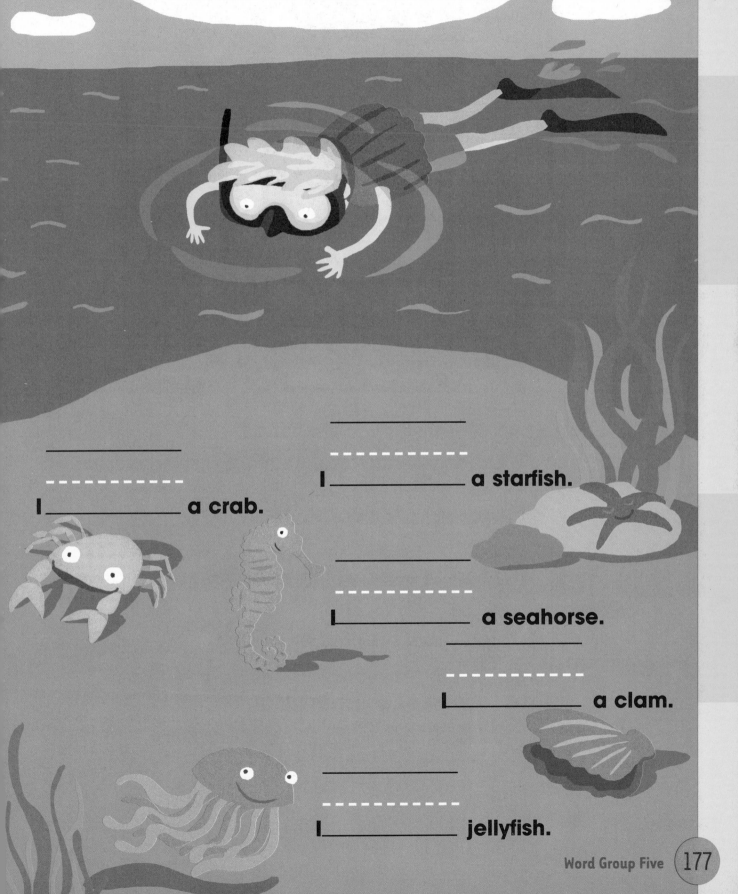

_____

I_____ a crab.

_____

I_____ a starfish.

_____

I_____ a seahorse.

_____

I_____ a clam.

_____

I_____ jellyfish.

Sentence Sense

Read the sentence.
Circle the word that makes the most sense.

I (can, see) my friends!

We (can, see) play in the park.

Do you (can, see) the big slide?

We (can, see) go down it fast!

We wave to our mothers and fathers.

Our mothers and fathers (can, see) us!

What Do You See?

Color the spaces with the word **I** green.
Color the spaces with the word **can** orange.
Color the spaces with the word **see** brown.
Color the spaces with the word **it** blue.

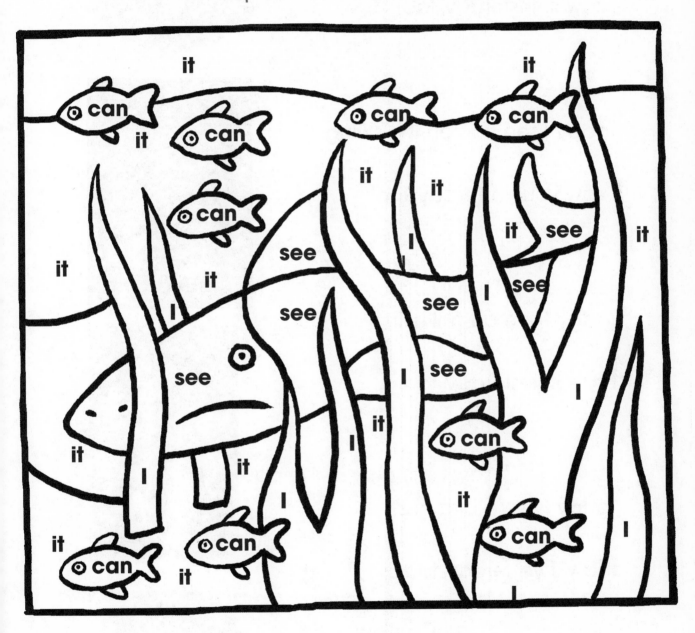

Which animal do you see? Circle the animal's name.

octopus   shark   clam

See, Saw

Draw a line to match the sentences with the pictures.

Today I see a spider web.

I saw it yesterday, too.

Today I see you on the swing.

I saw you yesterday, too!

Today I see an ant hill.

I saw it yesterday, too.

Today I see a bird nest.

I saw it yesterday, too.

Circle the word (see).
Underline the word <u>saw</u>.

Saw It!

Help the penguin cross the ice.
Color the ice floes that
have the word **saw**.

see

saw

see

saw

see

see

see

see

see

saw

see

see

see

see

saw

see

see

saw

see

see

saw

see

see

see

see

see

Now, draw a path from the penguin to his pals.

What the Explorers Saw

Help finish the story. Write the word **saw** on the lines.

The explorers walked in the jungle.

_____

They _____ monkeys.

_____

They _____ snakes.

_____

They _____ bugs.

_____

They _____ a tiger.

_____

The explorers _____ it was time to go!

What I Saw

Read the story. Circle the word that makes sense in the sentence.

Yesterday, we went to the beach.

I (see, saw) the ocean.

I (see, saw) a crab!

The crab did not (see, saw) me.

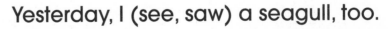

Yesterday, I (see, saw) a seagull, too.

The seagull (see, saw) my hot dog.

I did not (see, saw) the seagull near me.

The seagull ate my hot dog!

Monster Square

What are these monsters saying to each other?
Solve the monster square to find out.

①	r	h	c	e	a
t					a
a					s
t					t
e					n
u					m
r	e	o	a	s	y

The circled letter is written below.
Count three squares. Circle the letter.
Write that letter below. Keep going!
Count three squares and write the letter to
learn what the monsters are saying.

___ ___ ___   ___ ___ ___

- - - - - - - - -   - - - - - - - - - -

I ___ ___ ___   ___ ___ ___

___ ___ ___ ___   ___ ___ ___

- - - - - - - - -   - - - - - - - - -

___ ___ ___ ___   ___ ___ ___

___ ___ ___   ___ ___ ___ ___

- - - - - - - - -   - - - - - - - - - -

___ ___ ___   ___ ___ ___ ___ .

Build a Word

_____
- - - - - - - -
Write the word **a.** _____

_____
- - - - - - - -
a + t = _____

_____
- - - - - - - -
h + at = _____

_____
- - - - - - - -
t + hat = _____

Circle the word (**That**) in the sentences below.

That flower is white.

That bee is on the white flower.

That white flower is on an apple tree!

Word Group Five   187

This and That

Circle the word (This).
Draw a square around the word [That].

This ice cream is vanilla.

That ice cream is chocolate.

This cat is orange.

That cat is black.

This balloon is red.

That balloon is blue.

Draw a line to match each sentence pair with its picture.

This or That?

Put a ✔ on the picture that shows which one you want.

Do you want this fruit 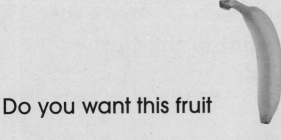 or that fruit  ?

Do you want this book  or that book  ?

Do you want this shirt  or that shirt  ?

Do you want this slice  or that slice  ?

Circle the word (this).
Draw a square around the word [that].
Underline the word **want**.

Monster Clothes

Help the monster pack for its trip. Write the word **want** below the clothes that have a ✓. Write the word **do not want** in the clothes that have an **X**.

Monster Trip

Write the word **want** on the lines.

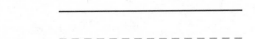

1. I  to sing.

2. I  to sleep.

3. I  to eat.

4. I to swim.

Write the number of the sentence next to the correct picture.

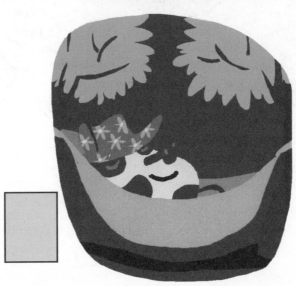

Let's Go!

Let's go to the party!

Let's go to the fair!

Let's go to the carnival—

See you there!

Let's go to the spaceship!

Let's go to the moon!

Let's go to the starry skies—

See you soon!

Circle the word **go**.
Draw a square around the word **to**.
Underline the word **the**.

Ready, Set, Go!

Who will win the race?
Draw an X on the word **go** to find out.

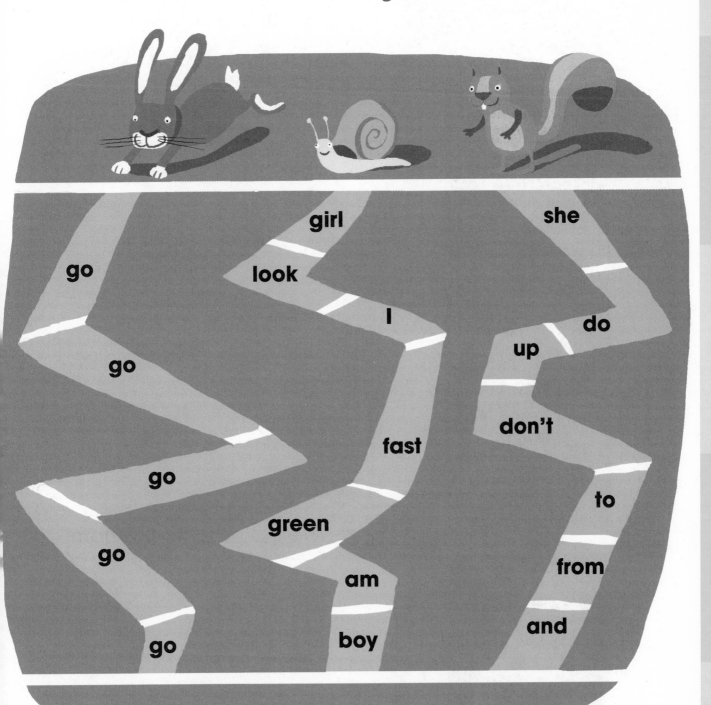

go

go

go

go

go

girl

look

I

fast

green

am

boy

she

do

up

don't

to

from

and

Who is the winner? Circle that animal's picture.

We Go

Write the word **go** on the line. Draw a line to match the sentence with the picture.

_____
- - - - - - - -
We _____ to school.

_____
- - - - - - - -
We _____ to the diner.

_____
- - - - - - - -
We _____ to the store.

_____
- - - - - - - -
We _____ to the park.

Vroom!

Write the word **car** to finish the sentences.

_____

- - - - - - - - - -

A _____ can go far.

_____

- - - - - - - - - -

There is a star on this _____.

_____

- - - - - - - - - -

That _____ is stuck in the tar.

_____

- - - - - - - - - -

There is a guitar on this _____.

_____

- - - - - - - - - -

This _____ must belong to a rock star!

Underline all the words that end with the same **-ar** sound as **car**.

A Sleepy Story

Write the word **book** to finish the story.

_____

- - - - - - - - - - - -

It was a good day to read a _____ .

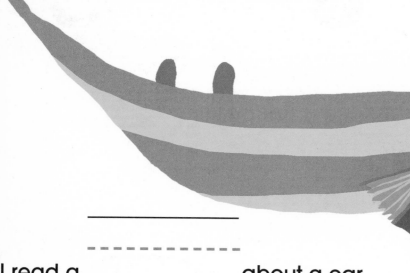

_____

- - - - - - - - - - - -

I read a _____ about a car.

_____

- - - - - - - - - - - -

I read another _____ about a cat.

I fell asleep.

_____

- - - - - - - - - - - -

One _____ was in my hand.

_____

- - - - - - - - - - - -

One _____ slid out of my hand.

I dreamed about a cat in a car.

What's black and white and read?

_____

- - - - - - - - - - - -

A _____ .

Old or New?

Put a ✔ in the right box to tell if the picture is of something old or new.

	old	new
	☐	☐
	☐	☐
	☐	☐
	☐	☐
	☐	☐
	☐	☐

Old Shoes, New Shoes

Circle the word (old).
Draw a star next to the word **new**.

I like old shoes,

old shoes like mine.

Old shoes feel fine.

I like old shoes!

I like new shoes,

new shoes like mine.

New shoes feel fine.

I like new shoes!

Which shoes do you like—old or new?
Draw your favorite shoes.

Sort the Socks

Sort the socks. Write the words from the socks in the correct basket.

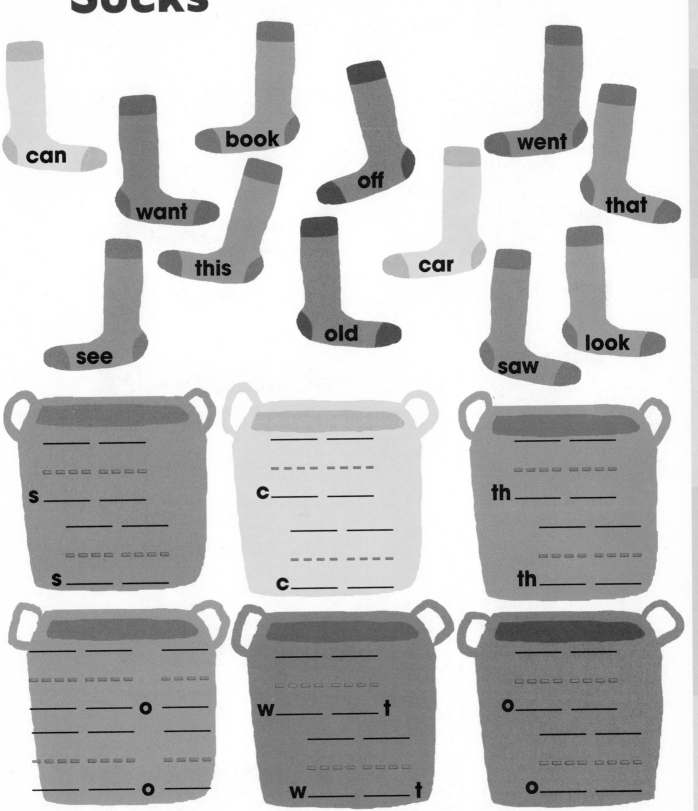

Matching Colors

Draw a line to match the color word
with the correct crayon.

black

blue

green

orange

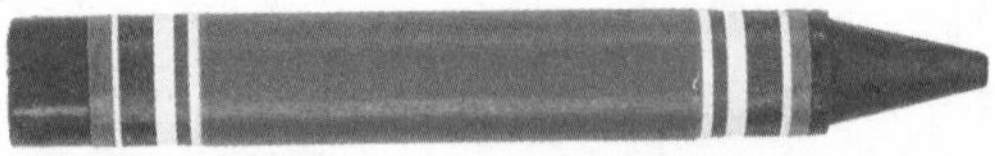

red

yellow

Colorful!

Read the color word.
Color the picture that color.

red

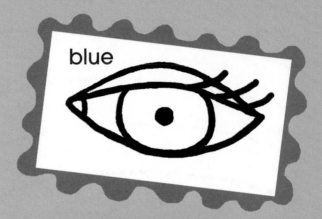

blue

yellow

black

green

orange

Rainbow Colors

Color the rainbow to match the color words.

red

red

red

orange

orange

yellow

yellow

yellow

green

green

blue

blue

blue

red

red

Fruit Colors

Use the words from the box to write the color of the fruits.

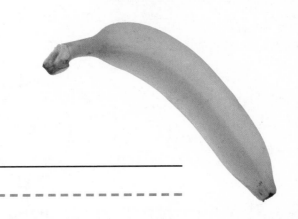

_____

\- \- \- \- \- \- \- \- \- \- \-

_____

_____

\- \- \- \- \- \- \- \- \- \- \-

_____

_____

\- \- \- \- \- \- \- \- \- \- \-

_____

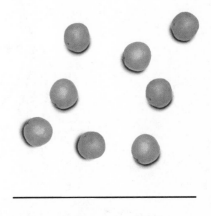

_____

\- \- \- \- \- \- \- \- \- \- \-

_____

_____

\- \- \- \- \- \- \- \- \- \- \-

_____

Favorite Color

What is your favorite color? (Circle) that color word below.

black   blue   green   orange   red   yellow

Color 3 balloons red.

Color 1 balloon black.

Color 2 balloons orange.

Color 1 balloon green.

Color 2 balloons yellow.

Color 3 balloons blue.

Let's Paint!

Write the correct color words on the paint can labels.

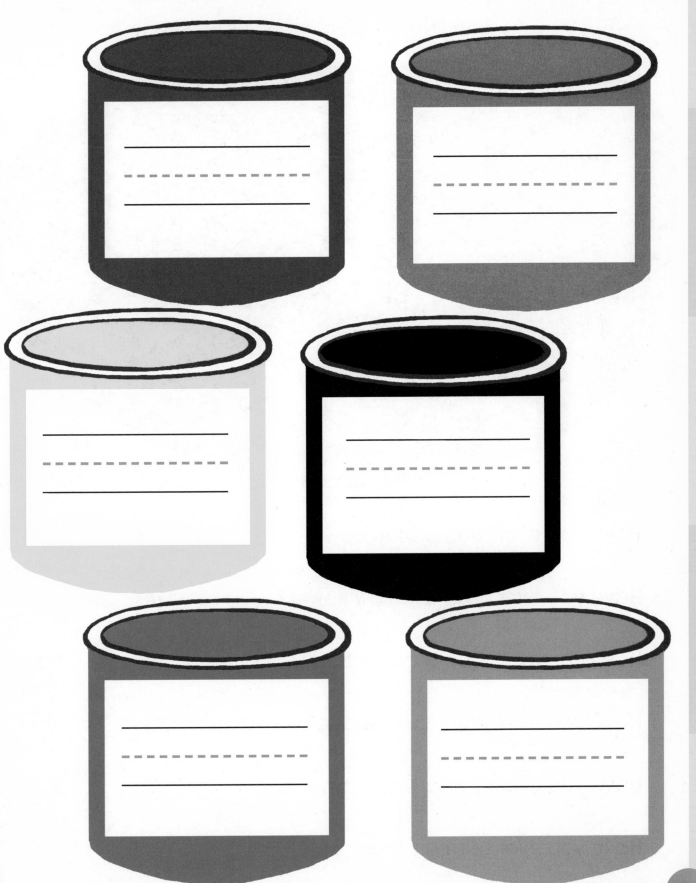

Have You Seen?

Circle the answers that make sense.

Have you ever seen a blue cow?	Yes	No
Have you ever seen a yellow flower?	Yes	No
Have you ever seen a green frog?	Yes	No
Have you ever seen a red sheep?	Yes	No
Have you ever seen a black moon?	Yes	No
Have you ever seen an orange pumpkin?	Yes	No

Nature Colors

Write the color word to tell the color of the things in the poem. The words in the box will help you.

Word Box

black   blue   green   orange   red   yellow

The _____ is _____ .

The _____ is_____ .

The _____ is_____ .

This all is true.

A _____ is _____ .

A _____ is _____ .

A _____ is_____ .

And that's a fact!

Desert Diamond

Help the explorer find the diamond.
Use the words in the sky to finish the puzzle.
Some letters have been filled in to guide you.
(Hint: Check the words off when you write them in the puzzles.)

can   car   black   blue   book   green
little   look   new   old   orange   rain   yellow
red   see   that   this   to   want   will

Color the diamond.
Write the word **saw** in the sentence.
Write the color word, too.

_____   _____

- - - - - - - - - - -   - - - - - - - - - - -
I _____ a _____ diamond.

Word Group 5 Answer Key

173 circle **can** 8 times; WELL DONE

174 a; an; can; write **can** 5 times; draw lines to match text to pictures

175 write **can** 4 times; circle **Can** 4 times; can; answers will vary

176 write **can** 5 times; draw lines to match text to pictures

177 write **see** 5 times

178 see; can; see; can; can, see

179 shark

180 draw lines to match text to pictures; circle **see** 4 times; underline **saw** 4 times

181 color **saw** 6 times

182 write **saw** 5 times

183 saw; saw; see; saw; saw; see

184 I can see that you are smart.

185 color flowers as directed; circle **this** 5 times

186 correct maze path follows word **this**

187 a; at; hat; that; circle **that** 3 times

188 circle **this** 3 times; draw a square around **that** 4 times; draw lines to match text to pictures

189 answers will vary; circle **this** 4 times; draw a square around that **that** 4 times; underline **want** 4 times

190 do not want; do not want; want; want; do not want; want

191 write **want** 4 times; numbers from top to bottom: 4; 3; 2; 1

192 circle **go** 6 times; draw a square around **to** 6 times; underline **the** 6 times

193 draw an X on **go** 5 times; circle rabbit

194 write **go** 4 times; draw lines to match text to pictures

195 write **car** 5 times; underline far, star, tar, guitar, star

196 write **book** 6 times

197 new; old; old; new; old; new

198 circle **old** 4 times; draw a star next to **new** 4 times

199 (order within pairs may vary) sit, saw; can, car; this, that; book, look; want, went; old, off

200 draw lines to match pictures to text

201 color as directed

202 color as directed

203 blue; yellow; green; orange; red

204 answers will vary; color as directed

205 from left to right: blue, red, yellow, black, green, orange

206 no; yes; yes; no; no; yes

207 yellow; blue; green; orange; black; red

208–209 see right; saw; green

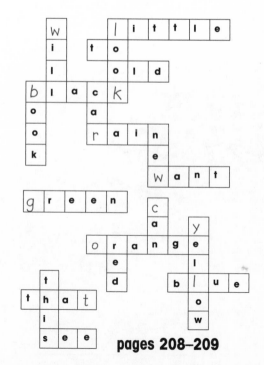

pages 208–209

Just then a little boy came in.

The boy saw Rainbow Bear.

But then he saw a new orange bear.

He looked at the orange bear.

He looked at Rainbow Bear again.

"I want this one," he said.

"Let's go home."

8

fold & assemble

Rainbow Bear

By Anne Schreiber

Illustrated by Greg Paprocki

Scholastic *100 Words Kids Need to Read by 1st Grade*, Word Group 5

1

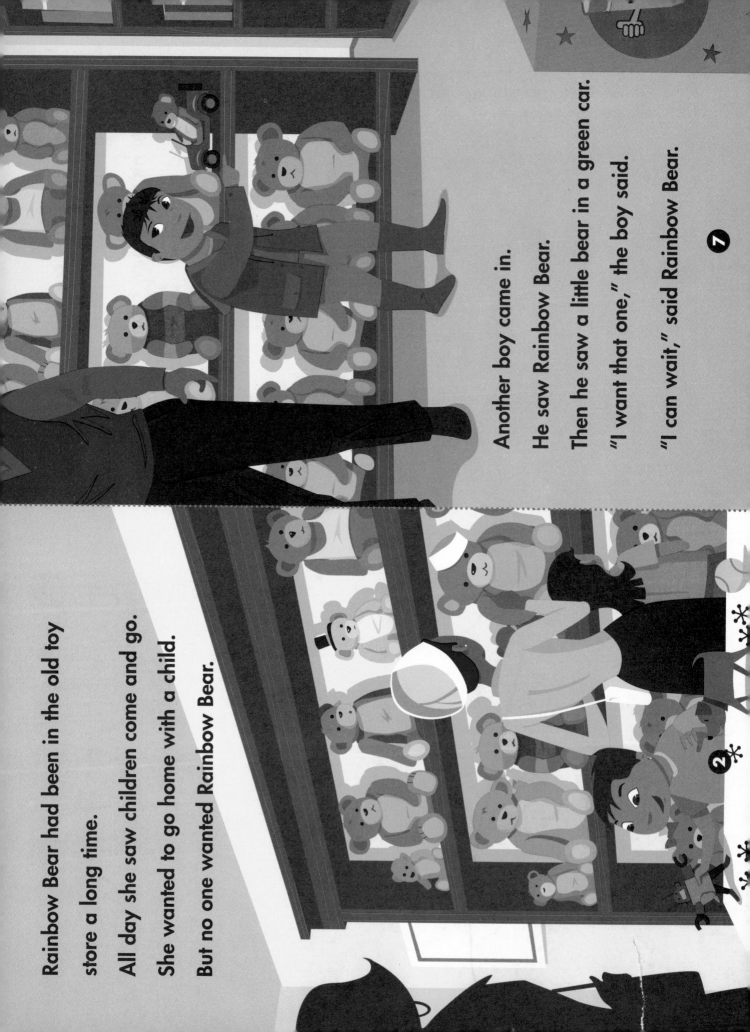

Another boy came in.

He saw Rainbow Bear.

Then he saw a little bear in a green car.

"I want that one," the boy said.

"I can wait," said Rainbow Bear.

7

Rainbow Bear had been in the old toy

store a long time.

All day she saw children come and go.

She wanted to go home with a child.

But no one wanted Rainbow Bear.

2

Another girl came in.

She did not even see Rainbow Bear.

She went right to a book about a bear.

"I want that," the girl said.

Now Rainbow Bear felt very sad.

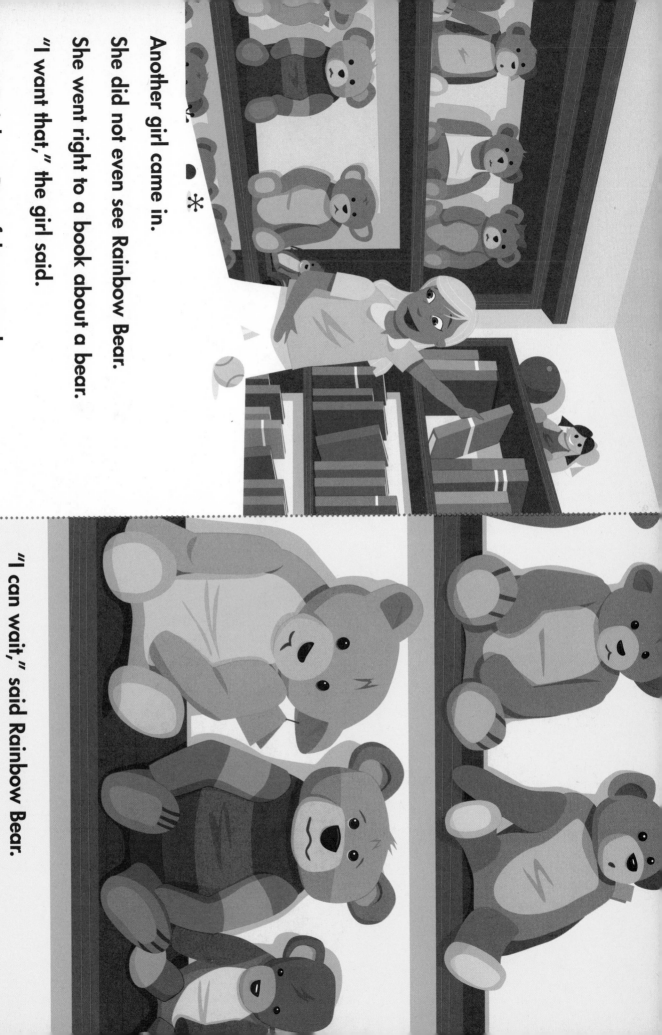

6

"I can wait," said Rainbow Bear.

"There must be a child who will want me."

3

A girl came in.

She looked at Rainbow Bear.

Then she saw a yellow bear.

The yellow bear had a new, black hat.

"I want that one," the girl said.

5

A little boy came in.

The boy saw Rainbow Bear.

Then he saw a blue and red bear.

"I want that one," the boy said.

4

Come, Harry!

My dog will come if I call him.

My dog will come if I say his name.

"Come, Harry!" I call to my dog.

And Harry will come!

Circle the word come in each sentence.
Then help the boy call his dog.
Write the word **Come** on the lines.

_____

- - - - - - - - - - - - -

_____ , Harry!

_____

- - - - - - - - - - - -

_____ to me!

_____

- - - - - - - - - - -

_____ with me for a walk.

Where Is Harry?

Help the boy find his dog, Harry.
Draw a line on the path that has the word **come**.

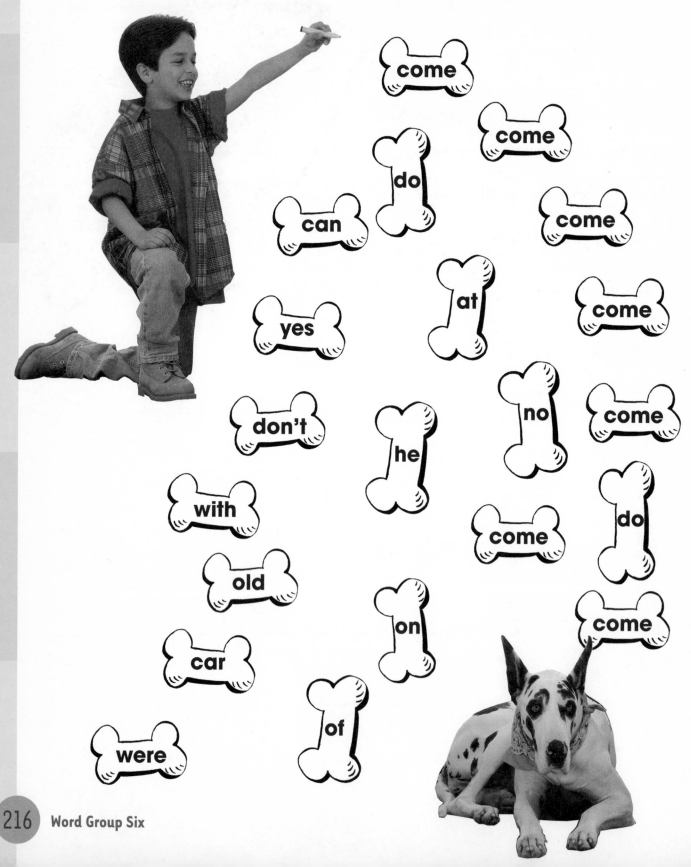

Come with Us

Write the word **Come** on each line.

_____
- - - - - - - - - - - - - -
_____ with us to the park.

_____
- - - - - - - - - - - - - -
_____ with us to the lake.

_____
- - - - - - - - - - - - - -
_____ with us to the beach.

_____
- - - - - - - - - - - - - -
_____ with us to the moon!

Draw a line to match the sentence
with the picture.

I Come, I Came

Put a ✓ next to what you did yesterday.
Put an X next to what you will do today.

Yesterday, I . . .	Today, I will . . .
_____ came to breakfast.	_____ come to breakfast.
_____ came to school.	_____ come to school.
_____ came home.	_____ come home.
_____ came to dinner.	_____ come to dinner.

Circle the word ⟨came⟩.
Draw a square around the word ☐come☐.

Who Came to My Party?

Read about the party. Write the word **came** on the lines.

Yesterday was my birthday.

I had a party.

_____

Tina _____ to my party.

_____

Maria _____ to my party.

_____

Alex _____ to my party, too!

_____

I was happy my friends _____ to my party.

Here, Kitty!

Help the firefighter get the cat out of the tree.
Fill in the letters on the ladder to spell the word **came**.

c __ __ __ __

c a __ e

__ a m __

c __ __ e

c __ m __

__ __ m e

Get the Balls

Help the baseball player hit a home run.
Find the baseballs with the word (get). Circle them.

Write the letters from the circled baseballs here:

—— —— —— —— —— ——

- -

—— —— —— —— —— ——

Unscramble the letters to write the words that tell
what the baseball player is trying to hit.

—— —— —— —— —— ——

- - - - - - - - - - - - - - - - - - - -

—— —— —— —— —— ——

Get Going!

Help the detective. Underline the footprints that have the word **get**.

yes

good

get

get

get

get

go

get

get

ten

get

get

SID

Get It?
Got It.
Good!

Draw a line to match the sentences with the pictures.

Let's go to the beach!

Did you get the towel?

I got it.

Good!

Did you get the pail?

I got it.

Good!

Did you get the ball?

I got it.

Good!

Circle the word get.

Draw a square around the word got.

Monster Gift

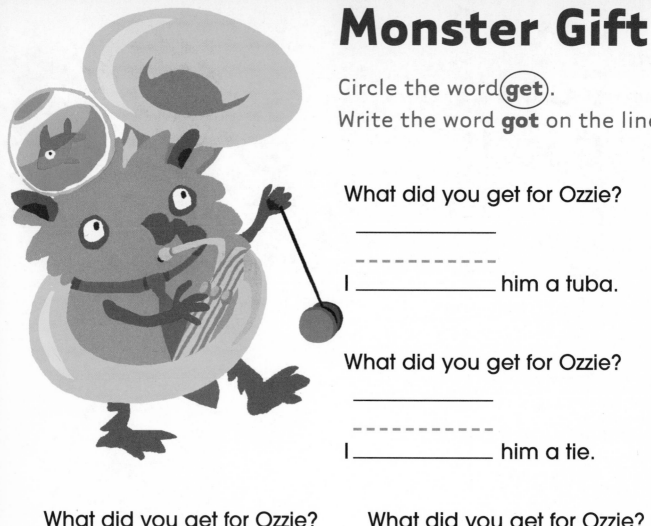

Circle the word (get).
Write the word **got** on the lines.

What did you get for Ozzie?

_____

I _____ him a tuba.

What did you get for Ozzie?

_____

I _____ him a tie.

What did you get for Ozzie?

_____

I _____ him a yo-yo.

What did you get for Ozzie?

_____

I _____ him a fish.

What would you buy
a monster? Draw your
monster gift. Write the
word **got** on the line.

_____

I _____ him a

Get Off!

Read the sentences. Circle the word that makes sense.

The cat **got** on lots of things.

Tom told the cat, "**Get** off!"

The cat (get, got) on the chair.

"(Get, Got) off!" said Tom.

The cat (get, got) on the table.

"(Get, Got) off!" said Tom.

The cat (get, got) in the sink.

"(Get, Got) out" said Tom.

The cat (get, got) on the counter.

"(Get, Got) off!" said Tom.

The cat got onto Tom's lap.

"Good cat," said Tom.

Dog Kisses

I give my dog food.

I give my dog water.

I give my dog a toy.

I give my dog a hug.

Circle the word give. Underline the word **my**.

Draw a star beside the word **I**. ☆

Write the word **give** on the line.

_____

- - - - - - - - - - -

My dog _____ s me kisses!

Our Best

Read the rhyme. Write
the word **give** on the lines.

_____

- - - - - - - - - - - - - - -

We _____ the teacher our homework.

_____

- - - - - - - - - - - - - -

We _____ the teacher our tests.

_____

- - - - - - - - - - - - - - -

We _____ the teacher our book reports.

_____

- - - - - - - - - - - - - -

We _____ the teacher our best.

What would you like to give your
teacher? Draw a picture of it.

Give Us a Cheer!

Write the word **give** on the lines to complete the cheer.
Write the letters of the cheer on the lines at the bottom.

us an R!

us a G!

us an E!

us an A!

us a T!

What does that spell?

_____ _____ _____ _____ _____

I Gave Him an Apple

The boy gave an apple to the giant. Color the spaces with the word **gave**.

girl	get	give	gave
got	give	gave	gave
good	gave	gave	goes
gave	gave	girl	give
gave	goes	got	give

I Gave

Circle the word **gave**.
Write the word **gave** on the line.

I gave my mom a flower.

_____

- - - - - - - - - - -

She _____ me a hug.

I gave my dad a sandwich.

_____

- - - - - - - - - - -

He _____ me a hug.

I gave my dog some water.

_____

- - - - - - - - - - -

He _____ me a lick.

I gave my cat a bowl of milk.

_____

- - - - - - - - - - -

She _____ me a rub.

230 **Word Group Six**

What Was It?

What did the boy give his brother? Color the spaces to find out. Color the spaces with the word **give** pink. Color the spaces with the word **gave** brown.

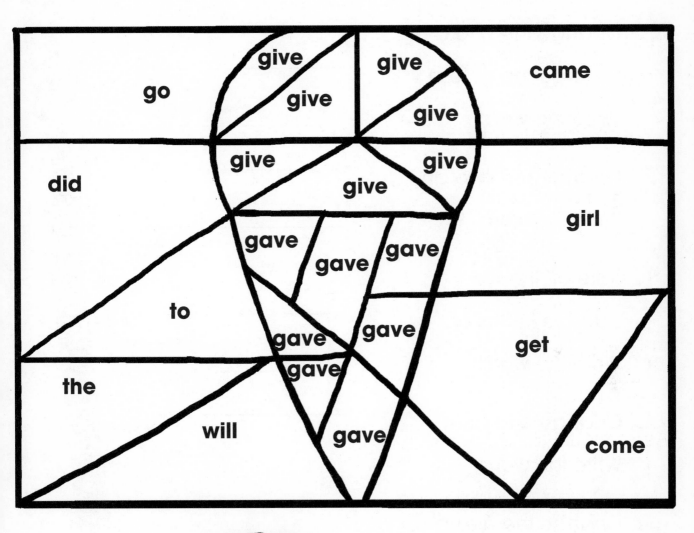

Word Changes

Follow the directions to change the words.

1. Write the word **came**.

2. Change the **c** to a **g**.

   Change the **m** to a **v**.

   Write the word.

3. Change the **a** to an **i**.

   Write the word.

4. Take off the **ive**.

   Add the letters **et**.

   Write the word.

5. Change **e** to an **o**.

   Write the word.

6. Change the **g** to a **c**.

   Change the **t** to **me**.

   Write the word.

7. Change the **o** to an **a**.

   Write the word.

One More Cheer

Read the clue. Write the new word on the line. (Hint: The words in the banner will help you.)

came   come   gave   get   give   got

Change one letter in **get**

Change one letter in **came**

Change one letter in **got**

Change one letter in **gave**

Change one letter in **give**

Change one letter in **come**

Write the cheer using the boxed letters above.

_____ _____ _____ _____ _____ _____ _____!

The Visit

Write the words in the sentences that make sense. The words in the box will help you. (Hint: One word is used twice.)

Word Box

came   come   gave   get   give   got

_____

My grandparents _____ yesterday!

_____

"We have _____ something for you," they said.

_____

"What did you _____ for me?" I asked.

_____

My grandparents _____ me a book!

_____

I _____ them a hug!

_____

I like when my grandparents _____ to visit!

_____

Next time, I will _____ them something.

Winning Words

Read the words in the race cars.
Find the words in the puzzle. Circle the words in the puzzle.

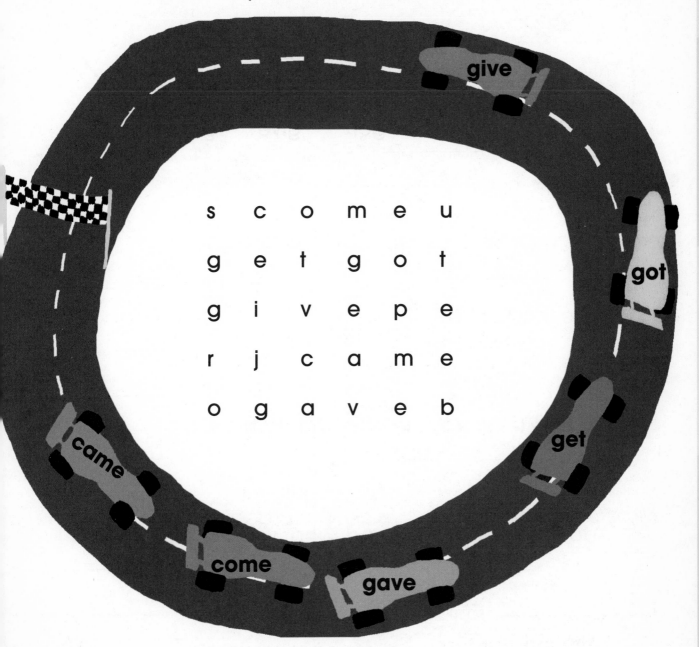

```
s   c   o   m   e   u
g   e   t   g   o   t
g   i   v   e   p   e
r   j   c   a   m   e
o   g   a   v   e   b
```

give

got

get

gave

come

came

Write the letters you did **not** circle on the lines,
in order, to read the hidden message.

___ ___ ___ ___ ___ ___   ___ ___ ___

--- --- --- --- --- --- ---   --- --- ---

___ ___ ___ ___ ___ ___

Make New Words

Write the word name next to each number.

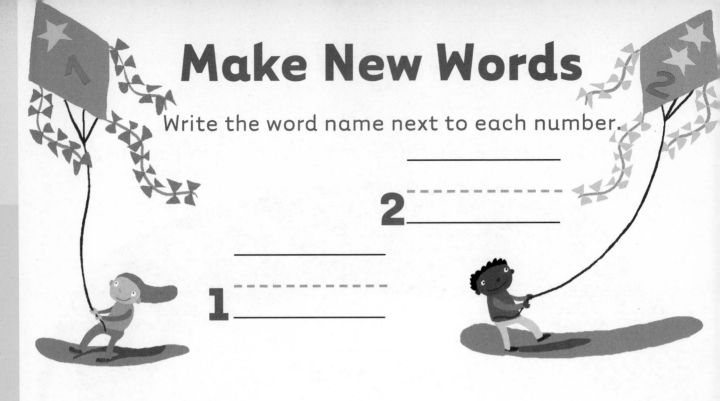

2 _____

1 _____

Make new words. Follow the directions.

1. Write the word **to**.

2. Add the letter **n** to the end and drop the **t**.

3. Add the letter **e** to the end. What word is it?

4. Write the word **to**.

5. Add the letter **w** in between the **t** and **o**.
   What word is it?

One and Two

Write the word **one** on the left line.
Write the word **two** on the right line.

_____

- - - - - - - - - - -

Here is _____ cat.

_____

- - - - - - - - - -

There are _____ cats.

_____

- - - - - - - - - -

I have _____ book.

_____

- - - - - - - - - - -

You have _____ books.

_____

- - - - - - - - - -

She has _____ hat.

_____

- - - - - - - - - -

Here are _____ hats.

Circle the words that end with
the letter **s** to show there is
more than one.

Three and Four

Write the word **three** next to the correct number.
Write the word **four** next to the correct number.

_____   _____

3 - - - - - - - - - - - - - - - -   4 - - - - - - - - - - - - - - - - - -

I see three ants!

Now there are four.

I see three butterflies!

Now there are four.

I see three ladybugs!

Now there are four.

I see three bees!

I don't want to see four!

Circle the word (three).
Draw a square around the word [four].

Party of Five

Write the word **five** next to the number.

_____

5_____

Happy birthday! Let's have a party!

Write the number word for how many things are on the table.

How many plates?
_____
- - - - - - - - - -
_____

How many forks?
_____
- - - - - - - - - -
_____

How many napkins?
_____
- - - - - - - - - -
_____

How many spoons?
_____
- - - - - - - - - -
_____

How many cups? _____

Do you see something with more than five? Circle it.

One, Two, Three, Four, Five!

Write the correct number word next to each number.
Then draw a line to match the number with the picture.

1 _____

2 _____

3 _____

4 _____

5 _____

Six and Seven

Color the fish that have **6** black stripes orange.
Color the fish that have **7** black stripes green.

Find the fish you colored orange.
Write the word **six** on the line below those fish.

Find the fish you colored green.
Write the word **seven** on the lines below those fish.

How many fish are on this page? Write the word.

Eight and Nine

Write the word **eight** next to the correct number.
Write the word **nine** next to the correct number.

_____   _____

8 _____   9 _____

Write **8** on the shirts with the word **eight**.
Write **9** on the shirts with the word **nine**.
Now, color the shirts with the word **eight** one color.
Color the shirts with the word **nine** another color.

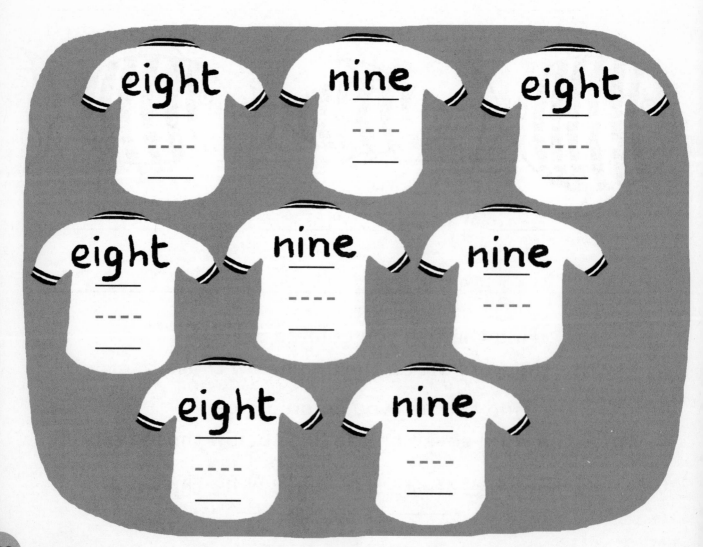

Ten Friends

Circle the word (ten).
Write the word **ten** on the line.

_____
- - - - - - - - - - - -

Ten friends have _____ cats.

_____
- - - - - - - - - - -

Ten friends have _____ hats.

_____
- - - - - - - - - - -

Ten friends have _____ trucks.

_____
- - - - - - - - - -

Ten friends have _____ ducks.

How many children do you see?

_____   _____
- - - - - - - -   - - - - - - - - - -

Write the number. _____   Write the number word. _____

Six, Seven, Eight, Nine, Ten!

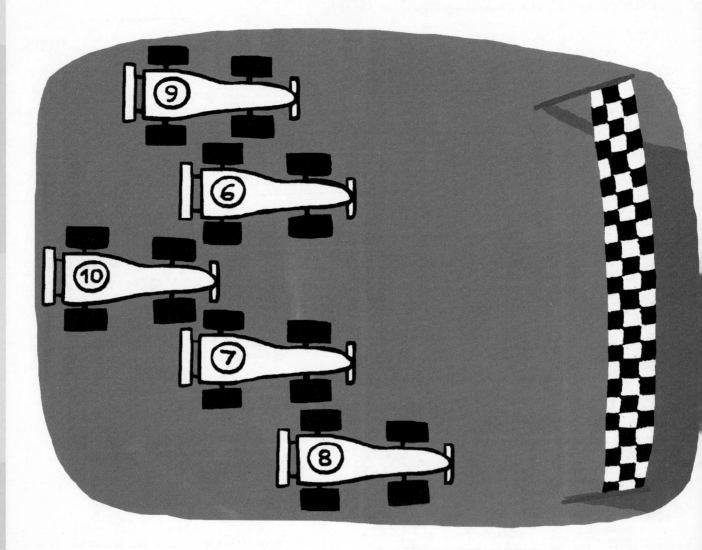

Color the **six** car blue. Color the **seven** red.
Color the **eight** car yellow. Color the **nine** car green.
Color the **ten** car orange.
Which car is winning? Write the number word.

_____

....

_____

Animals On Top

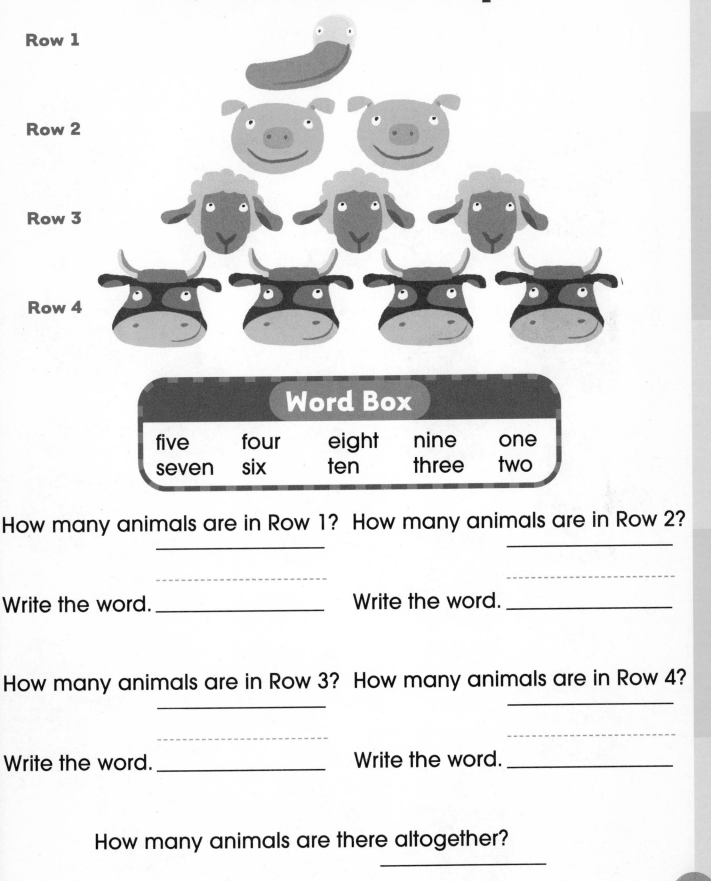

Row 1

Row 2

Row 3

Row 4

Word Box

| five | four | eight | nine | one |
| seven | six | ten | three | two |

How many animals are in Row 1?

_____

Write the word. _____

How many animals are in Row 2?

_____

Write the word. _____

How many animals are in Row 3?

_____

Write the word. _____

How many animals are in Row 4?

_____

Write the word. _____

How many animals are there altogether?

_____

Write the word. _____

Pair Up!

Draw a line to match the number word in one mitten with the number in another mitten.

Buggy!

Write the number word in the spaces.

_____

1 _____

_____

6 _____

_____

3 _____

_____

2 _____

_____

10 _____

_____

4 _____

_____

8 _____

_____

5 _____

_____

9 _____

_____

7 _____

Going Sailing

Lift the sails!
Connect the dots, from **one** to **ten**.

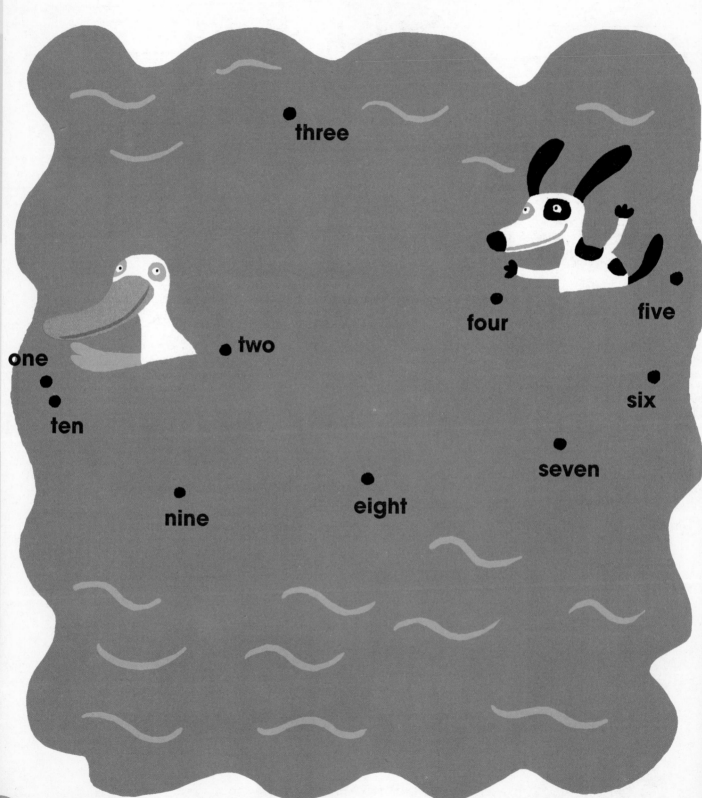

three

four

five

two

one

six

ten

seven

nine

eight

The Classroom

Use the words from the box to answer the questions.

Word Box

five	four	eight	nine	one
seven	six	ten	three	two

1. How many children are in the class? _____

2. How many teachers are in the class? _____

3. How many books are on the shelf? _____

4. How many posters are on the wall? _____

5. How many backpacks are on the floor? _____

Counting Down Rhyme

Circle the number words.
Write the number word that finishes the rhyme.

Come along.

Let's have some fun.

Let's both count from

Ten to one.

There are ten flowers,

growing in a line.

If we pick one, _____

- -

There will be _____ .

Look! Eight kites,

flying high as heaven.

One hits a tree. _____

- -

Now there are_____ .

Here come six bees

out of a hive.

One buzzes back in.

_____

- - - - - - - - - -

Now there are_____ .

Four birds are singing,

up in a tree.

One flies away.

_____

- - - - - - - - - -

Now there are_____ .

We have two balls,

We're ready for fun.

A ball rolls away.

_____

- - - - - - - - - -

Now there is _____ .

We like counting

from one to ten.

Let's start at one

and do it again!

Word Group 6 Answer Key

215 circle **come** 4 times; write **Come** 3 times

216 maze path follows the word **come**

217 write **Come** 4 times; draw lines to match text to pictures

218 answers will vary; circle **came** 4 times; draw a square around **come** 4 times

219 write **came** 4 times

220 a, m, e; m; c, e; a, m; a, e; c, a

221 circle 7 baseballs; HOME RUN

222 underline 8 footprints

223 circle **get** 3 times; draw a square around **got** 3 times; draw lines to match text to pictures

224 circle **get** 4 times; write **got** 5 times; picture will vary

225 got, get; got, get; got, get; got; get

226 circle **give** 4 times; underline **my** 4 times; draw a star beside **I** 4 times; give

227 write **give** 4 times; give; picture will vary

228 write **give** 5 times; GREAT

229 color 8 spaces with **gave**

230 circle **gave** 4 times; write **gave** 4 times

231 ice cream cone

232 came; gave, give; get; got; come; came

233 got; come; get; give; gave; came; go team

234 came; got; get; gave; gave; come; give

235 see right; super job

236 one, two; to; on; one; to; two

237 one, two; one, two; one, two; circle cats; books; hats

238 three; four; circle **three** 4 times; draw a square around **four** 4 times

239 write **five** 5 times; circle the candles on the cake

240 one; two; three; four; five; draw lines to match text to pictures

241 six; seven; seven; seven; six; six; six

242 eight; nine; write **8** 4 times; write **9** 4 times; colors will vary

243 circle **ten** 4 times; write **ten** 4 times; 10; ten

244 color as directed; eight

245 one; two; three; four; ten

246 draw lines to match numbers and words

247 one; six; three; two; ten; four; eight; five; nine; seven

248 one-two-three-four-five-six-seven-eight-nine-ten; dots form a sail

249 five; one; eight; two; three

250–251 circle: ten, one; ten, one; eight, one; six, one; four, one; two, one; write: nine; seven; five; three, one

page 235

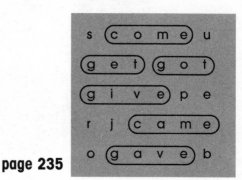

One tiny toad gave a yawn and said,
"It is fun to give a party."
Then he climbed into bed.

8

fold & assemble

Toad Party

by Kathryn McKeon

Illustrated by Valeria Petrone

Scholastic *100 Words Kids Need to Read by 1st Grade, Word Group 6*

1

The ten toads sang songs.

They had lots of fun.

Then nine toads went home.

Now there was just one.

One tiny toad gave a party.

Two toad friends come over.

Now there are three.

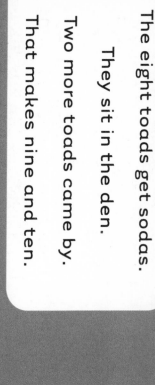

The eight toads get sodas.

They sit in the den.

Two more toads came by.

That makes nine and ten.

6

The three toads hear a bang on the door.

One toad came inside.

Now there are four.

3

The six toads got a cake.

They ate it on one plate.

Two more toads came by.

That makes seven and eight.

5

The four toads play a game with sticks.

Two more toads came by.

That makes five and six.

4